WHO'S WATCHING THE PLAYPEN?

David Benoit

First printing—Fall '95—10,000
Second Printing—Fall '96—5,000

All references are from the King James Version unless otherwise stated.

Who's Watching the Playpen?
Copyright © 1995 by David Benoit

Printed in the United States of America

Published by:
Hearthstone Publishing, Ltd.
500 Beacon Dr. ● Oklahoma City, OK 73127
(405) 787-4055 ● (800) 580-2604 ● FAX (405) 787-2589

Cover design by Eric Ferguson.
Line drawings by Virginia Boyter.

ISBN 1-57558-000-4

I want to dedicate this book to my three sets of parents
who prepared the course of my life:
My biological parents—Ernest and Mary,
my stepparents—Dr. George and Pat Arnold,
and my wife's parents—LaMar and Glendora Forsyth,
who taught my wife to live a godly life.

Special thanks to Randy and Carole Smith—
without their help this book would not
have been written.

Table of Contents

Section IV—Encouragement for the Christian

Introduction

MISSING THE OBVIOUS LOOKING FOR THE SUBTLE

For years I have spoken out against the effects of rock music. I've spoken on the blatant Satanism and anti-Christian themes that pour out of these musicians' mouths. I've had the privilege of ministering to millions of parents and teens on the obvious dangers of rock music on our society. As I look back on the years I spent exposing the obvious themes of rock music, it wasn't until I started talking about the subtle that I drew the crowds.

In the mid-1980s I started exposing backward masking. Subliminal messages about the Devil were easily heard when the records were played backward. I used a special record player that ran forward and backward to reveal these hidden messages in the music. The auditoriums were filled with crowds of people who were drawn to my meetings. Secular radio and television stations sent reporters to cover the events. And yes, we had many people make professions of faith in Christ.

Then one day my machine broke. When pastors heard I no longer had a record player to expose the backward masking in rock music, they no longer wanted to hear my message on rock music. The sad part about this is that the pastors didn't want to hear about the obvious, they wanted to shock people with the subtle.

During this time, the New Age media had a heyday. They were telling people how stupid Christians were for believing in subliminal motivation, while at the same time they were selling billions of dollars worth of subliminal tapes which they claimed could cause you to quit smoking and eating. I personally believe that subliminal motivation works. It has been proven. Did you know that it is illegal to put even one frame in a movie telling people to buy coke and popcorn? It's illegal because in studies done, the number of people responding to the subliminal message was great enough to cause concern.

I am not writing this chapter to convince you of the subtle. Instead, I want to warn you about missing the obvious. I learned two things from my experience with backward masking in the 1980s.

1. When Christians go after the subtle, the world considers them radical, unbelievable, and reactionaries.
2. Once people are shocked by the subtle, they lose interest in the obvious. This is my concern.

In the mid-1980s literally hundreds of people were doing rock seminars like mine, exposing backward masking. Today you are hard pressed to find even a handful of people who do rock music seminars.

Now the Devil is at it again. Just a few weeks ago I spoke at a Christian school convention and the place was buzzing with people talking about *The Lion King*. Numerous people walked up to me and said, "Mr. Benoit, did you know that when Simba hits the ground in the movie *The Lion King*, the dust particles spelled out s-e-x?"

My response was, "Yes, I saw the letters s-e-x come together near the left-hand side of the set and quickly disappear."

I also said, "Did you see the witch doctor? Did you see Simba talk to his father who was dead? Did you see Rafiki in a yoga position?" (For more information on subliminal messages by Disney, see Section I.)

To tell you the truth, I am more concerned about our children bonding themselves to a witch doctor than I am about them seeing the letters s-e-x develop out of leaves.

The 1980s backward masking became a joke. Rock musicians started to deliberately put hidden messages on their albums to sell records. Don't be surprised if you start hearing that more subliminal messages are being found. It may become another marketing tool to sell movies.

In conclusion, let me express my concern. I'm concerned that Christians today will be so preoccupied looking for the hidden, they will accept all kinds of demonic and evil messages that are right there in front of them! So if the Lord tarries for a few more years, ministries like mine will have to shock people with the obvious while they are blinded by the subtle!

Section I

ENTERTAINMENT FROM HOLLYWOOD

WHO PREPARED
THE CHICKEN JOUP?

*Understanding Dr. Jack Canfield,
the Educator*

By now you have probably heard of the delicious new book called *Chicken Soup For the Soul* and its sequel, *Second Helping*. It's now in the top ten on the *New York Times* best seller's list. *Chicken Soup For the Soul* is being sold in Christian bookstores, is recommended by Sunday school teachers, and is even being given as gifts to pastors.

Chicken Soup For the Soul and *Second Helping* each have a collection of 101 uplifting stories of strength and courage. As a matter of fact, the very first story was written by Mother Theresa. The book has been recommended by success guru Anthony Robbins, as well as other notable people in the field of education and self-help. Before you run out and purchase a few copies for you and your pastor, maybe we ought to look at the "chef" who prepared this tantalizing meal for the soul.

Dr. Jack Canfield is co-author of this book. Maybe you would like to know a little bit about his background. First of all, he holds the title of director for the Institute of Holistic Education, according to a Canadian publication, *The Editonion Journal*. The following is a quote from the October 11, 1979, edition of that journal. It was written by Marilyn Moysa and is entitled "Improving Images Seen As a Key To Help."

> Imagine more than eight hundred of North America's top judges, lawyers, education professors, social workers, and just plain parents chanting an Indian mantra. Even Meyer Horowitz, University of Alberta president, sang along in the guitar-accompanied chant. "Whatever happened to the keynote address?" I kept asking myself. Wasn't this supposed to be the big opening number of a national conference on children with learning disabilities? What happened, quite simply, was Jack Canfield, director of the Institute for Holistic Education in Amherst, Mass. . . . Images, claims Dr. Canfield, can have power beyond the will of an individual when it comes to change.
>
> The article then shows how Canfield took a learning disabled sixth grade girl and had her go through guided imagery with a "wise old woman" up a stairway of light. Through this, the girl discovered the meaning of life. The

eight hundred lawyers and educators applauded this profound experiment and its insight.

Tal Brooke is a man whom I highly respect as a researcher. In his book, *When the World Will Be As One*, he tells how Jack Canfield and his co-director, Paul Klimek, exposed their educational intent.

Canfield's extremely long feature article in the *New Age Journal* is packed with materials, techniques, and insights. Canfield and Klimek state that New Age education has arrived and that more and more teachers are exposing children to ways of contacting their inner wisdom and higher selves.[1]

The Canfield and Klimek article entitled "Education In the New Age" was published in the *New Age Journal*. A quote from that article will help you to understand why I am concerned about this world renowned "chef" of *Chicken Soup For the Soul*.

Within the past five years, we have also witnessed the birth of "transpersonal education," the acknowledgment of one's inner and spiritual dimensions, through working with such forms as dreams, meditation, guided imagery, biofeedback, centering, mandalas, and so forth. Now is the time to combine both of these focuses, for the New Age means integrating the soul and personality ... [and] views the student as being engaged in an integral process of unfoldment under the direction of his/her higher self. This process is perceived as taking place in a universe that is also constantly evolving: each of us is seen as an important part of the larger planetary and universal evolution of consciousness.[2]

Dr. Jack Canfield is not opposed to using the media to accomplish this evolution of your child's soul.

> A wonderful way to do this, we have found, is to use the tools the media are providing. An example might be to ask, What's this thing called the force in *Star Wars*? How does Luke communicate with it? How does it help him? The next question is, Well, would you like to have this kind of experience? (The answer is always an overwhelming "Yes!") Well, we can try this and see what happens. There are some ground rules you will need to follow. At this point, the kids are more than ready. The media has done a lot of the work for us.[3]

By the way, *Star Wars* was produced in 1978. This article was written in 1978. Timing is important for the New Age teaching.

So, parents are being duped by the media into setting up their own children so they can be seduced in the class room.

Maybe you're saying, "Tell me no more, David. I loved the book *Chicken Soup For the Soul*. I gave the book as a gift to a friend. Say no more, David!" Well, I must. Let's look at one more quote from the *New Age Journal*.

> We believe that guided imagery is a key to finding out what is in the consciousness of New Age children. . . . Children are so close to spirit if we only allow room for their process to emerge. We celebrate to fantasize what is in store for all of us. . . . Additional emphasis in the transpersonal dimension are using nature as teacher, and aligning and communicating with other kingdoms such as the elemental and divine realms. . . . Working with children's psychic capacities (such as seeing auras); working with astrological charts. . . . The souls that are pres-

ently incarnating seem to be very special.[4]

After reading these quotes, many of you may be confused with the terms used. So let me give meaning to some of the words in order to help you understand Dr. Canfield's basic beliefs.

Transpersonal education. This is a recent educational theory which advocates that students must go beyond the realm of the five senses into the transpersonal realm which allegedly takes people to a higher source of knowledge, wisdom, and ability. In essence, it means to be transformed from the natural senses to the supernatural.

One's inner and spiritual dimensions. The New Age teaches that there is an inner core of man which needs to be awakened. Realization is a big buzz word in the New Age movement. It means you have always been god, you just didn't realize it. Getting in touch with your inner self is tapping into your godship.

Guided imagery. This is a technique used by New Age therapists or counselors to guide their patients into using their imaginations to bring something into reality. At first, the counselors guide them into visualization, then they introduce them to spirit guides (a New Age term for demons) who are eagerly waiting to "possess" them, not "guide" them.

Biofeedback. According to the dictionary, this is "a technique in which an attempt is made to consciously regulate the bodily functions thought to be involuntary, such as blood pressure, by using an instrument to monitor the function and to signal changes in it." This sounds quite natural and normal. I believe that stress and cares do cause us physical problems, but people in the occult will use it as a means of going into altered states of consciousness. Make sure that the person performing biofeedback is a qualified person with the right equipment, not a snake charmer.

Centering. This is a cover-up word for meditation. Centering is often used by New Age teachers who do not want parents to know they are teaching meditation to their children. Other cover-up words for meditation are relaxation exercise, visualization, and holistic learning, to name a few.

Elementals. The belief that nature can be altered by the will of man. The five elementals used by witches are earth, wind, fire, water, and spirit. The Bible warns us of false teachers who seem to be loving, gentle, and kind, but inwardly are vile.

> Beware of false prophets, which come to you in sheep's clothing, but inwardly they are ravening wolves (Matt. 7:15).

As you look at *Chicken Soup For the Soul,* understand that even though the stories may be heartwarming, they are for the soul. The soul is a spiritual thing. Now that you understand how Dr. Canfield views the soul, you can see that his belief is contrary to what Christians believe.

After speaking in a church the other day, a young man who was an employee of a Christian bookstore realized that he was selling this book to the Christian community. He reviewed it and found several things that Christians should disagree with.

1. **"Rules for Being Human,"** p. 81—"Your answers lie inside you." We have already discussed Dr. Canfield's belief in the inner man. The Bible says, "I can do all things through Christ which strengtheneth me" (Phil. 4:13). We know that the flesh will fail us, but Christ never will.

2. **"The Golden Buddah,"** p. 69—This represents

a story which the author learned from a golden Buddah. But what does the Word of God say about this?

What profiteth the graven image that the maker thereof hath graven it; the molten image, and a teacher of lies, that the maker of his work trusteth therein, to make dumb idols? Woe unto him that saith to the wood, Awake; to the dumb stone, Arise, it shall teach! Behold, it is laid over with gold and silver, and there is no breath at all in the midst of it. But the LORD is in his holy temple: let all the earth keep silence before him (Hab. 2:18–20).

3. **"Two Monks,"** p. 289, **was the wisdom of Zen Masters.** Again, Zen Buddism is a false religion. How does this book find its way into the Christian market?

4. **Cartoon of two birds in a tree,** p. 112— There is nothing wrong with the cartoon, except it was reprinted by permission of *Playboy* magazine. I wonder how this great spiritual guy happened to stumble onto this picture?

5. In one story, **the reader is told to love the one creative force.** We do not love a "creative force," we love the almighty God who created us. Deuteronomy 6:5 says, "Thou shalt love the LORD thy God with all thine heart, and with all thy soul, and with all thy might." May the name of the Lord be lifted up forever!

Scripture teaches that good and evil are diametric opposites invested in the personal characters of God and Devil. Occultism and witchcraft teach that good and evil are invested in a neutral, primordial force, whose moral quality depends on the motive of the individual. Thus, white witches can claim to use the same power as black witches, except they propose to avoid her.

In the *Star Wars* epic, Darth Vader and Luke Skywalker both use the same force, but their motives are different. This concept makes good and evil opposite sides of the same spiritual coin, since both derive their energy from the same source. The notion of the force is derived from pantheism and is contrary to the Christian view.[5]

I find it interesting that in the King James Version of the Bible, Daniel 11:38 tells us this about the Antichrist:

> But in his estate shall he honour the God of forces: and a god whom his fathers knew not shall he honour with gold, and silver, and precious stones, and pleasant things.

Strangely enough, the new translations interpret this verse, "He will honor the god of fortresses."

Yes, you can read the book *Chicken Soup For the Soul,* and have good, religious feelings. But you need to know Dr. Jack Canfield's background and where he's coming from. Dr. Canfield is not a good, wholesome man with Christian values oozing from his book. If he were, his book would not be on the *New York Times* best seller's list. Why do I say this? Dr. James Dobson is well-known in Christian circles. If his book, *Dare To Discipline,* which has sold over two and a half million copies, can't make the *New York Times* best seller's list, then neither will any other books that emphasize true Christian values.

So be warned. Someone may have poisoned the soup!

THE LION WHO
WOULD BE KING

If I were to tell you that the Bible talks about a lion who is referred to as a king, could you give me his name? If you said Simba, you are wrong! The king I was referring to is Jesus.

Revelation 5:1–5 says:

> And I saw in the right hand of him that sat on the throne a book written within and on the backside, sealed with seven seals. And I saw a strong angel proclaiming with a loud voice, Who is worthy to open the book, and to loose the seals thereof? And no man in heaven, nor in earth, neither under the earth, was able to open the book, neither to look thereon. And I wept much, because no man was found worthy to open and to read the book, neither to look thereon. And one of the elders saith unto me, Weep not: behold, the Lion of the tribe of Juda, the Root of David, hath prevailed to open the book, and to loose the seven seals thereof.

There is more than just one correlation between the Lion King of Judah and *The Lion King* of Disney. Before we make those correlations, let's look at how the selection of a king became a rejection of God.

> Then all the elders of Israel gathered themselves together, and came to Samuel unto Ramah, And said unto him, Behold, thou art old, and thy sons walk not in thy ways: now make us a king to judge us like all the nations. But the thing displeased Samuel, when they said, Give us a king to judge us. And Samuel prayed unto the LORD. And the LORD said unto Samuel, Hearken unto the voice of the people in all that they say unto thee: for they have not rejected thee, but they have rejected me, that I should not reign over them (1 Sam. 8:4–7).

As you can see, it was never God's plan to have a king. It was the plan of some very carnal men who wanted to imitate the world. They wanted to be ruled from below instead of from above.

We must understand that every time someone replaces God, it is a serious thing. The question that may be running through your mind right now is, "What does this have to do with a harmless cartoon produced by Disney?" Let's take a look at this "harmless" cartoon.

The Anointing of *The Lion King*

One of the very first scenes you see in *The Lion King* is that of a beautiful kingdom of animals running in jubilant anticipation of the birth of the new king. It is very easy to get lost in the beautiful music and the magnificent artwork. The sun shines brightly above the animals as they stand at attention. Their new king is about to be revealed.

Then the camera takes you in close for the anointing. Rafiki carefully anoints the head of the new king and then lifts up the lion cub so that the whole kingdom can pay homage to their king who will keep peace in the kingdom.

Here are a few problems that Christians ought to have with this:

1. There is only one true King that can and will bring peace on this planet, and that King is Jesus.

2. The one that anointed Simba as king was Rafiki. Have you ever stopped to think that Rafiki is a witch doctor? Throughout the whole movie he carries his staff with his magical pack tied to the top. When Simba runs away Rafiki discovers that Simba is alive by taking materials out of the air that Simba came into contact with. He mixes it with his magic potion and announces that Simba is alive.

Even today, law enforcement agents consult psychics who claim they can find the lost if they can only come into contact with something which that lost person owned or had come into contact with at some point. This is not a gift these psychics have. It is a demonic spirit that has the knowledge of the lost person's whereabouts.

One scene in the movie shows Rafiki in an altered state of consciousness with his legs crossed, his eyes closed, and his fingers together. You might say to me that the scene only lasted seconds. Yes, that is correct, but isn't it interesting that that scene is in almost every book put out on *The Lion King*? You must understand that reinforcement is important in the New Age movement. If you remember, Leonardo was in an altered state of consciousness in the movie *The Teenage Mutant Ninja Turtles*. That is how he contacted Splinter, his Zen Master, so he could rescue him. Was that scene a harmless throw-away scene, or was it a vivid picture in the minds of children?

Just a couple of months ago I was in a church where

the pastor stood up after my message and told a very interesting story to the congregation. He and his son of about
six years of age were walking. All of a sudden his son fell to
the ground, crossed his legs and put his fingers together.
Immediately the pastor asked his son, "Where did you learn
to do that?" The son replied, "Rafiki did it."

This boy comes from a Christian home, his dad is a
pastor, he attends a Christian school, and yet he watched
The Lion King only one time and picked up on that one
scene to re-enact. Needless to say, this alarmed the pastor
and made him immediately aware of how some New Age
images can infiltrate his godly home through so-called
"harmless" entertainment. If that could affect this young
boy who comes from a strong Christian home and a good
Christian school environment, can you imagine how it could
affect a child who comes from a home that never has devotions, attends a public school where New Age teachers reinforce New Age meditation, and has seen *The Lion King*
thirty to forty times!

Jack Canfield instructs teachers of children to use the
media to reinforce New Age doctrine. So, in essence,
throughout the whole movie the audience is taught that
you can align yourself with witchcraft to overcome evil. In
the occult this is called white magic. In the Bible it's called
an abomination.

In 1 Samuel 10:1 we read about the anointing, "Then
Samuel took a vial of oil, and poured it upon his [Saul's]
head, and kissed him, and said, Is it not because the LORD
hath anointed thee to be captain over his inheritance?"
The first king of Israel was Saul and he was anointed by
Samuel, a godly man who walked with God, not a witch
doctor.

The Anointed Simba
Anyone who saw *The Lion King* has to admit that the

character was cute, lovable, and very easy to relate to. He was funny and fun-loving. Yet, he was cunning, mischievous, and disobedient to his father. There was something interesting about this because occultists teach that Jesus was also capable of all the sins that youth have, such as lying, deceiving, and craftiness.

The truth is, Jesus, the Lion King of Judah, was sinless. He never disobeyed His heavenly Father, nor was He ever drawn away by youthful lust. We have no record of the first twelve years of Jesus' life. We don't know at what age He started to walk, and His first words were not recorded. As Bible believers, we have no record of Jesus' childhood. Yet, in the occult they may call these years the hidden years—a time when Jesus was taught by the Druid priests who were masters in the art of magic. Maybe Simba was taught by the masters because, you may remember, he was ordained by the witch doctor. But Jesus was ordained by God. Had Jesus been disobedient to His parents He would not have been sinless. Jesus was sinless from birth to death. Had He sinned He would not have been able to die for our sins.

The obvious question is: Didn't Jesus, in Luke 2:42–49, disobey His mother and father by being in Jerusalem? The answer is no. Jesus was not cunning, crafty, nor disobedient to His parents. There is no record of them forbidding Him to stay in Jerusalem. He was there in obedience to His heavenly Father, not in disobedience to His earthly parents.

Why should I be concerned about making analogies between a cartoon character that no one takes seriously, and Jesus who is the King of kings? *The Lion King,* just like *Star Wars,* had people coming out of the theaters feeling good about themselves spiritually. That alarms me!

Recently, a pastor of a large Southern Baptist church preached a message to his congregation on the topic, "Be

Happy." The entire message was an analogy drawn from the movie *The Lion King*. He even showed slides from the movie during his message.

Not long ago I received a phone call from a concerned mother who needed information on *The Lion King* to present to her child's teacher. This teacher saw nothing wrong with *The Lion King* and, in fact, showed the movie to her entire class. She was a Christian teacher in a Christian school!

The Addressing of the Dead

There shall not be found among you any one that maketh his son or his daughter to pass through the fire, or that useth divination, or an observer of times, or an enchanter, or a witch, Or a charmer, or a consulter with familiar spirits, or a wizard, or a necromancer. For all that do these things are an abomination unto the LORD: and because of these abominations the LORD thy God doth drive them out from before thee (Deut. 18:10–12).

The word *necromancy* means talking to the dead. The practice has always been condemned in the Word of God and condoned in the art of witchcraft. That is basically what Halloween is all about: talking to the dead. Occultists believe that tradition teaches that the veil between the natural and the supernatural is at its thinnest during Halloween. Movies like *Ghost* and *The Lion King,* to name a few, teach people it is possible to gain help from the dead. This is totally false. The rich man in Luke 16:22–28 who died and went to Hell could not help his brothers see. People who try to contact the dead through seances, Ouija boards, and psychics have not contacted the dead at all. They have contacted what the Bible calls "familiar spirits." The reason they are called "familiar" is because these demons imitate people you are trying to contact. They become familiar to you. Even the angel at the grave of Jesus asked, "Why seek ye the living among the dead?" (Luke 24:5).

Surely Christians would not promote talking to the dead. Or would they? I was doing a live interview program with two Christian psychologists and the question came up, "What could be wrong with *The Lion King?*" I replied that in the movie they teach talking to the dead. "Remember when Rafiki takes Simba to talk to his father? His father appears to him from the dead and tells Simba to remember who he was." The Christian psychologist quickly responded by saying that there is no scripture that tells us not to talk to the dead. He went on to say, "As a matter of fact, I often advise my clients who are grieved at death to go to the grave and talk to their loved ones."

What he was telling me is that talking to the dead is helpful in the grieving process. However, I was not talking about telling your father, who is dead, that you are sorry for your rebellion. Rather, I was talking about your father saying back to you from the grave, "It's okay, I forgive you." Simba's father was dead, yet he told Simba to remember who he was.

Can *The Lion King* have a negative effect on your child's belief about death? Last weekend I spoke at a Christian school convention. A teacher shared with me a story about another Christian school teacher who worked with her. She said that the teacher's husband recently died and her son is having a hard time accepting the fact that his father will not talk to him from the dead like Simba's father did.

If *your* husband suddenly died, what would *you* tell your child if he asked the question, "Why can't Daddy talk to me from the dead like Simba's father?" Most parents would tell their children that what Simba did was make-believe; that people don't really talk to the dead. The problem with that answer is that millions of Americans believe they can talk to the dead. This is not make-believe. It's a religious belief called "necromancy." How dangerous it is for us, as parents, to think that moviemakers like Disney just put these things in for entertainment. They purposely use religious beliefs for indoctrination, not for entertainment.

Another example of this occurred when I was doing a television program. We had a live studio audience provided to us by a local youth group. Again I told the audience that I had a problem with Simba talking to his dead father. One of the members of the live audience wrote me a note and it read like this: "Mr. Benoit, what is wrong with Simba talking to his father who was in Heaven? Didn't Jesus talk to His Father who was in Heaven?"

Now I thought that was a well-thought-out question, so I responded with a well-thought-out answer. "Yes, Jesus did talk to His Father in Heaven, but Jesus' Father is God, not someone who was killed on this planet and made it to Heaven."

You see, whether it's deliberate or not, people are still making analogies to this movie with a spiritual undertone. Individual analogies may not be bad, but the problem is that when you consider the whole picture, it is contrary to the Word of God.

The Allurement of the Antichrist

The basic story line in *The Lion King* is that the kingdom is looking for a one-kingdom leader, someone who comes bringing peace, life, light, and joy to the world.

Today the people of the world are being primed in very subtle ways to receive a one-world leader. It seems that all advertisements are trying to make us think global. When Mikhail Gorbachev came to America, he said we needed a one-world government. The masses gave him standing ovations. We have not had a one-world government since the tower of Babel and now the world is calling for it. The Bible tells us that there will be a one-world government and its leader is called the Antichrist. We are given a pretty vivid picture of a vile, wicked man in Daniel 11:36–39:

> And the king shall do according to his will; and he shall exalt himself, and magnify himself above every god, and shall speak marvellous things against the God of gods, and shall prosper till the indignation be accomplished: for that that is determined shall be done. Neither shall he regard the God of his fathers, nor the desire of women, nor regard any god: for he shall magnify himself above all. But in his estate shall he honour the God of forces: and a god whom his fathers knew not shall he honour with gold, and silver, and with precious stones, and pleasant things. Thus shall he do in the most strong holds with a strange god, whom he shall acknowledge and increase with glory: and he shall cause them to rule over many, and shall divide the land for gain.

1. He will be a humanist; a self-worshiper.
2. Like Shirley MacLaine, he will claim to be God.
3. He will be a God-hater.
4. He will hate those who love God.

When he comes on the scene the Antichrist will seem to have sunshine, joy, peace, and tranquility for the world. Instead, he will bring the judgment of God on this planet.

I must admit, the writer of *The Lion King* is very clever. A king was produced that Christians could cheer for and see nothing wrong with, in spite of the fact that he was ordained by a witch doctor and he talked to the dead. Then, to top it off, if a minister says something bad about *The Lion King*, he is condemned as a radical. Disney, let me tip my hat to you. I wish I could make Christianity as appealing to the lost as you make witchcraft appealing to the Christians!!

ARE THE POWER RANGERS MORPHING YOUR CHILDREN?

To the best of my knowledge, the word *morph* means to "change" or "transform." So in essence, the question being asked is, Has your child been "changed" by the Power Rangers? Here are some easy test questions to see if your child has been morphed:

O **Has your child become more aggressive and violent?** This is becoming an increasing problem among children today. Young people are becoming more violent. *The Charlotte Observer,* October 17, 1994, Oslo, Norway:

> No one knows if the Mighty Morphin Power Rangers had a role in the death of a 5-year-old girl who was stoned and kicked by playmates and left to freeze in the snow, but the networks didn't take any chances. The Scandinavian network, TV3, moved quickly Tuesday to drop the wildly popular U.S. children's show from its broadcasts in Norway, Sweden, and Denmark in response to debate over violence in children's programs.

The Charlotte Observer, November 3, 1994, Toronto:

Beating up on Rita Repulsa may not be too violent for American children to watch, but it is proving too much for the Canadian elementary set. Spurred by an industry council's finding that the Mighty Morphin Power Rangers depicted excessive violence, a Canadian television network pulled the children's show from the airwaves this week.

Isn't it strange that Norway, Sweden, and Canada—countries not necessarily known for their long heritage of Christian values—have said no to violence while America—known around the world as a Christian nation—sees nothing wrong with it? Does this kind of television affect the Christian home? The answer is: Absolutely!

Recently at a Christian school convention where I was speaking, a second grade teacher shared this observation with me. "I have taught elementary school students for years but something is starting to alarm me. It used to be that children would play on the slides, swings, and teeter-totter. Now these things sit idle while the children involve themselves with martial combat using martial arts-style kicks and punches." Many Christian schools have had to ban the bringing of toys and clothing that represent the Power Rangers because they incite young people to violence.

Not long ago a concerned grandmother in West Virginia asked me to pray for her grandson. She told me that he is about three years old and walks around the house saying, "I'll kill you. I'll cut you up." He watches a lot of the Mighty Morphin Power Rangers. Another Christian lady approached me about the violent tendencies in her young son. The worried mother told me that when he doesn't get his way, he pretends he has razor blades for fingers and pretends to cut her up. That leads me to my second stage of the morphing of your children.

○ **Does your child reject your authority?** One of the predominate themes in children's programs is that children are right and parents are incompetent. That is exactly the same thing Hitler told his youth movement. He told them that the parents had failed and it was up to children to save the race.

It used to be that children honored their parents. According to the Bible, this is right. Humanists have taken all the rights away from the parents and given them to the children. Today children are suing their parents. Some are even killing their parents.

In Romans 1:30–31 the Bible describes a person given over to a reprobate mind. They are "backbiters, haters of God, despiteful, proud, boasters, inventors of evil things, disobedient to parents, Without understanding, covenant-breakers, without natural affection, implacable, unmerciful."

A few things may need to be pointed out from this passage to help you understand just how subtle your child's morphing may be. A backbiter is a person who verbally inflicts wounds on people. Does your child have a quick mouth that often leads you, as a parent, to say, "Who taught you that?" or, "Don't you ever let me hear you say that again"? Is your child filled with spite? There's a big difference between a strong-willed child and a spiteful child. Does your child love the things of God? Are church and Sunday school boring to your child? Are your children disobedient to you as a parent? Are they without natural affection? "Without natural affection" means to have no natural love for the family. Do you find your child making statements like: "When I become eighteen, I'm getting out of this house" or, "I wish I had never been born into this family"?

I realize that these are piercing questions, but are your children living in rebellion at a preteen age? Maybe that's by design. It might just be that they are being morphed, or transformed, right in the comfort of your own living room.

The word *implacable* is a Greek word that means, "I will not surrender." It's a warrior's term that means under no condition will they ever surrender. The Power Rangers are great teachers of this principle. Day after day, Power Rangers are willing to die before they surrender.

The sad part is that young Rangers around the world find themselves with the same dedication as their super heroes. An example of this was found in *USA Today,* October 19, 1994. The article was entitled "Power Ranger Tommy Is Reborn."

Jason Frank was getting a little old to play a Power Ranger. (You must understand that they deliberately want young people as role models, not adults.) So they were going to kill off Jason Frank, who at that time was the Green Ranger. There was only one problem. Children had already bonded so tightly to Jason's character, he became indispensable. So Fox turned him from the Green Ranger to the White Ranger. (I will discuss the meaning of the colors in another chapter). "Viewers' complaints streamed in. One kid said he was never going to eat again if I didn't come back," Frank says.

You may call it a childhood imagination. I call it a very sincere commitment. Are your children committed to you and your family, or are they committed to an imaginary family of Power Rangers?

○ **Do your children have a problem distinguishing the difference between fantasy and reality?** If so, they may have been morphed. Anton LeVay, the founder of the Satanic Church, says the best way to get a person into the occult is through fantasy. The question that may arise now is, "Didn't you, as a child, play cops and robbers, or cowboys and Indians?" Yes, I did. And yes, I pretended to shoot the bad guys but, that was different. Let me explain:

1. When we were growing up, the cops and robbers were adults. As kids we could not totally identify with the characters. Today, television bombards children with images of children doing the killing, not just adults. So children today see that as "normal." They can totally relate to that character. We are seeing a rise in violent crimes performed by younger children, such as the case with the small children who killed the 5-year-old girl in Norway.

2. Television today is more graphic in its depiction of killing. When we were growing up, we saw an Indian shot off a horse. You heard the blast and saw the Indian fall. Today not only do you hear the blast, you actually see the person's face deteriorate as you pull the trigger. The cameras in old films were second person. You saw someone else shoot people. Now the camera is first person. The camera angle puts you behind the gun barrel. You become the killer.

America's teens are in trouble and we need to come back to reality. Every 30 minutes in America 29 teens will attempt to commit suicide, 23 teenage girls will have abortions, 685 teens will become regular drug users. Not all of this can be blamed on parents and bad homes. The media must take responsibility for its actions.

○ **Are your children having a problem believing in God as their source of power?** If they are, they may have been morphed. *Man, Myth and Magic* defines morphic resonance this way:

The theory of evolution by natural selection, first

propounded by Charles Darwin and now regarded as dogma by most organisms, developed gradually over many generations. A small genetic change results in a modification of the organism, which is subsequently transmitted to its offspring; if this modification is favorable to its survival, giving it an advantage over its relatives, and is succeeded by further favorable modifications, it will result in the organism's eventual domination.[1]

Basically, what is said here is that God did not create animals. Evolution is capable of explaining God away. It simply means the creatures adapt to their environment. From the beginning, the Power Rangers have used evolution as their source of power and strength. Red Ranger morphs, or transforms, into Tyrannosaurus Dinozord. Yellow Ranger morphs into Sabertooth Tiger Dinozord. Black Ranger morphs into Mastodon Dinozord. Blue Ranger morphs into Triceratops Dinozord. Pink Ranger morphs into Pterodactyl Dinozord.

Darwin taught that the strong survive. The Bible teaches that the meek shall inherit the earth. You will not find the word "morph" anywhere in the Bible, but you will find the word "transformed."

Romans 12:1–2 says:

I beseech you therefore, brethren, by the mercies of God, that ye present your bodies a living sacrifice, holy, acceptable unto God, which is your reasonable service. And be not conformed to this world: but be ye transformed by the renewing of your mind, that ye may prove what is that good, and acceptable, and perfect, will of God.

My prayer is that your children will be transformed by God's Word, not morphed by some Power Rangers.

POWER RANGERS—
THE BEASTS FROM WITHIN

From the very beginning I had a problem with the Power Rangers calling on spirits of dinosaurs. Now they no longer need the help of the dinosaurs. They, themselves, have become gods. Let me explain.

In *The Mighty Morphin Power Rangers, the Movie,* an evil villain named Ivan Ooze is set free by accident. His vengeance is aimed toward Zordon, the leader of the Power Rangers. Zordon is empowered by crystals (which I thought was interesting because New Agers believe crystal power can be a sustainer of life). While the Rangers are fighting Ivan the Ooze's hatchet men, Ivan goes to the Power Rangers' command center and destroys it. With the destruction of the command center they have lost their powers and no longer have super-hero strength. What will they do? There is only one hope. They must leave this planet and be transported to a planet called Phaedos so they can find the great powers of Phaedos. The power they were seeking was the powers of the Ninjetti. It was to be found in the Temple of the Great Power which was in the center of the pyramid.

For those of you who are unaware of the pyramid power, it's the powers of the ancient spirit of Egypt. The philosophy of pyramidology is based on the idea that the ancient Egyptian pyramid of Cheops was built according to precise geometric measurements and alignments to channel an unexplained biocosmic force, or electromagnetic field.[1] I don't claim to know much about an imaginary place called Phaedos, but I do have a little knowledge of Egyptology and the two seem strikingly similar.

While the Power Rangers are on that planet they meet a female warrior named Dulcea who gives the Rangers a new source of power. These new spirits will make their dinosaur powers seem prehistoric. It's now time for your child to know the new powers. The powers of the dinosaurs reinforced in your child the belief of evolution which explains away the one true God. Your child is now ready for Phase II of those magnificent morphers. Now the Mighty Morphin Power Rangers are out to reinforce in your child that they can become gods. You may ask how this can be done. Let me show you.

Dulcea leads the Rangers to a Stonehenge replica and introduces them to their Ninjetti animal spirits. She says,

"Aisha, you shall be the bear, fierce and unstoppable. Rocky, you are the mighty ape. Billy, you shall be the wolf, cunning and swift. Kimberly, you are the crane, agile and light as a feather. Adam, you are the frog, patient and wise. And Tommy, you are the falcon, lord of the skies."

Why were these specific animal spirits chosen from the entire animal kingdom? That was my question, so I went to the library and researched these animals. I found all but one listed in the occult encyclopedia of information called *Man, Myth and Magic* (*MMMagic*). What I found may interest you:

○ **The bear, fierce and unstoppable.** Dulcea will tell you that an angry bear will attack its victim with an unbelievable vengeance. I have had the opportunity on several occasions to visit the beautiful state of Alaska. I've heard the horror stories of bears who have attacked people. It's not a pretty sight. Even during the Roman Empire when they used crucifixion as a mode of entertainment, bears would sometimes be released to tear Christians off the cross. "Bear festivals are celebrated in parts of Europe."[2]

Not only in Europe are these creatures worshipped, but also in the American Indian culture. "Northern Indians killed bears for food but always apologized to the dead animal for the indignity, since it was thought that the bear possesses great supernatural powers, even to be a god in disguise. So the bear's head and hide would be ceremonially laid out, and care would be taken with the bones (so that the bear would not be crippled in the spirit world). The Kootenay Indian in the Canadian Rockies believed in a group of bear gods who could be prayed to for help."[3]

The strangest bear story is associated with the she-bear. Oddly enough, Aisha is a she-bear. "The legend of the bear woman is fairly common among North American Indians and among other primitives, too. Usually it involves a tribesman who marries a strange woman with special magical powers and finds that she is a bear able to take human form."[4]

The bear is also found in Revelation 13:2. It is part of an unholy trinity of animals empowered by the Dragon. Nowhere is the bear a symbol of good in the Christian faith, except when the bear will be tamed during the Millennium.

○ **The ape.** Rocky is the mighty ape. In my research I didn't come across the ape in a part of worship as are the other spirits of the Power Rangers. In parts of Africa, however, the great ape is probably worshipped. Keep this in mind: the Power Rangers used to get their power from the spirit of dinosaurs, which was a way the humanists reinforced to your children the belief in evolution. The Rangers have now gone from the evolution of the body to the evolution of the spirit. Now comes the final stage of this evolution process, moving toward being gods. Becoming a god is not a new concept in the Devil's bag of tricks. In the Garden of Eden, Satan told Eve that she could become as God. Genesis 3:5 says, "For God doth know that in the day ye eat thereof, then your eyes shall be opened, and ye shall be as gods, knowing good and evil."

The ape, as one of the Power Rangers' new spirits, may be the link between man and gods. So, in essence, the humanist still may want children to look toward the missing link, or the ape if you will, to explain the evolution of this god called man.

○**The wolf.** Billy is now the wolf, known for his ability to be swift and cunning. Among the Greek gods and goddesses, no other animal had more reverence appeal:

   a. The priests of Zeus were believed to have the ability to turn into a wolf.
   b. Hecate also could take the shape of a wolf.

    c. Leto (who is supposed to be the mother of Apollo) and Artemis were supposed to be transformed into she wolves.

    d. The Roman's associated the wolf as a god of war.

    e. "In Scandinavian mythology, the fenris wolf is one of the three children of Liki, the others being the midgard serpent and Hel (Deuth). Fenris, the wolf, whose jaws stretched from heaven to earth, created much trouble among the gods until they managed to bind him with a magic cord."[5]

In Germany, the wolf is associated with the Devil. According to German myth, witches ride wolves as well as turn into them. You also have the werewolf that is supposed to be able to transform a man into a wolf.

As we move from myths to reality, we find the wolf as a predator who has an appetite for sheep. Just like the bear, the wolf would often find sheep easy prey. The shepherd would often have to guard and protect his sheep from the wolf. Jesus knew how cunning and vicious wolves could be. In Matthew 7:15, He warns the early Christians about this: "Beware of false prophets, which come to you in sheep's clothing, but inwardly they are ravening wolves." This can also be a warning for children today. Outwardly, Billy may seem nice, friendly, and also cool. But inwardly he may be the prince of violence which may lead children away from the Prince of Peace.

○ **The crane.** Kimberly is now the crane, known for its agility and light weight. "St. Columbia, who was called 'crane cleric,' was said to have turned some women into cranes."[6] Cranes are long-necked birds and, like the falcon, are associated with the worship of the sun god Ra.

A crane dance was performed by human dancers in

ancient Crete in connection with Labyrinth, the home of the minotaur. The layout was circular and apparently the performance was enacted in an arena of swastika patterns. The circle and the swastika are both symbols of the sun. We may assume that the dance was a solar ritual, which is in agreement with evidence that the crane was a bird of the sun.[7]

In the Far East, crane dancers were associated with a group of ideas, thunder, rain, fertility and reincarnation.[8]

Finally, the crane is linked to the Taoist funeral ceremonies. (It's also from the Taoist belief that we get the yin yang that Jason wears around his neck). Ra is supposed to be the sun god, the giver of life. We do not believe that. As Christians, we believe that Jesus Christ is the true giver of life. John 10:10 says, "The thief cometh not, but for to steal, and to kill, and to destroy: I am come that they might have life, and that they might have it more abundantly."

○ **The Frog.** Adam is the frog spirit. He is supposed to be patient and wise. The legend of the frog is filled with imagery of magic. For example, who hasn't heard the story of the prince who was turned into a frog? Who hasn't seen the witch at the cauldron adding the frog to her special brew? Those are, of course, the legends of the frogs. But did you know that frogs were used in medicine until the seventeenth century? People have claimed that a frog could cure a tooth ache, protect your orchard, help people with epilepsy, even lower a fever. When I was growing up, if you had warts they were said to have been caused by frogs. The frog is a part of the zodiac in Japan. It is worshipped in the Hindu religion for its ability to bring rain.

The Chinese call the frog the "celestial chicken." Probably the culture that had the strongest belief in the frog as deity was the Egyptian culture. God plagued the Egyptians in Exodus 8:1–14 because they worshipped a goddess named Hekt. This goddess was a fertility goddess that was represented by the frog. God is going to attack Hekt again in Revelation 16:12–14:

> And the sixth angel poured out his vial upon the great river Euphrates; and the water thereof was dried up, that the way of the kings of the east might be prepared. And I saw three unclean spirits like frogs come out of the mouth of the dragon, and out of the mouth of the beast, and out of the mouth of the false prophet. For they are the spirits of devils, working miracles, which go forth unto the kings of the earth and of the whole world, to gather them to the battle of that great day of God Almighty.

That's right. The dragon, which is the Devil, will have the frog spirit proceeding out of his mouth, as well as the Beast and the False Prophet. If you read verses 1–5, you will find that this spirit of the frog will help them prepare for the greatest battle of all, Armageddon. "And he gathered them together into a place called in the Hebrew tongue Armageddon" (Rev. 16:16).

O **The falcon.** Tommy is the falcon, or lord of the skies. The White Ranger is now the falcon, chief of all the gods. "Because the sun so insistently dominates the daily scene in Egypt, it was venerated under the name Re (Egyptian coptic for 'sun') as the supreme state deity, intimately associated with the monarchy. Known as the 'Great God,' Re was conceived under various highly imaginative forms. Re-Horakhti, an ancient falcon or falcon-headed sky god called 'Horus of the Horizon' was associated with the sun god."[9]

What we've been seeing here is a perversion of the

Creator's original plan. Didn't He tell Adam and Eve to take dominion over the earth and bring every living thing under their authority?

> And God blessed them, and God said unto them, Be fruitful, and multiply, and replenish the earth, and sub-due it: and have dominion over the fish of the sea, and over the fowl of the air, and over every living thing that moveth upon the earth (Gen. 1:28).

How is it, then, that the mind of man could become so twisted and perverted that he reversed God's order and placed himself in subjection to the animals? Romans 1:21–23, 25 has the answer.

> Because that, when they knew God, they glorified him not as God, neither were thankful; but became vain in their imaginations, and their foolish heart was dark-ened. Professing themselves to be wise, they became fools, And changed the glory of the uncorruptible God into an image made like to corruptible man, and to birds, and fourfooted beasts, and creeping things . . .Who changed the truth of God into a lie, and worshipped and served the creature more than the Creator, who is blessed for ever. Amen.

Like the frog, the sun was worshipped in Egypt. Jeho-vah sent ten plagues upon the Egyptians to let them know that He was God. These ten plagues had a fourfold pur-pose:

1. To show Israel their God was the true God.
2. To show the Egyptians their gods were false.
3. To harden Pharaoh's heart which would lead him to his own destruction.

4. To release His people from the bondage they were in.

The plague against the sun god Re, or Ra, was held until the ninth plague. Exodus 10:22 tells us that darkness was over the land for three days. You have to understand, the sun god was their greatest god, and now the land of Egypt was covered with darkness for three days. Those ten plagues were designed by God to free His people so that they could worship Him. Today, God is preparing another exodus for his people and soon He will judge this planet and those who worship it instead of Him.

Yes, the children are awestruck by the new Ninjetti spirits of the Mighty Morphin Power Rangers. Yes, they believe that the Power Rangers are gods. You may ask how I can say that. Easy. Only God has the power to raise the dead, right? At the end of the movie, Zordon is dead but the Rangers realize they have all power. They again combine their powers to raise Zordon from the dead.

This chapter is not to say that animals are bad. God does not hate wolves; He created them. God does not hate frogs; He created them. God does not hate cranes, apes, or falcons. God spared the animal kingdom by telling Noah to build an ark large enough to house them all. God could have killed every animal in the flood and saved 120 years of Noah's time. But God loves His creation. He created all things and said it was good. All of God's creatures were made the same in God's eyes. New Agers elevate these creatures to deity. The Power Rangers do not imitate these animals, they are supposedly empowered by the spirits of these animals.

This chapter is not to make you protest zoos in America. When my children were small, we took many trips to the zoo. My prayer is that the gods of the Power Rangers will not harden the hearts of your children toward Jehovah, the one true God. I hope that your children will not be recruited by the Antichrist to make war with the saints.

POWER RANGERS—
COLORING THEIR WORLD

Satan is a master weaver. He prides himself on the fact that he is able to weave evil material into good material without being detected. One example is color. Can you imagine life without color? God uses color to show His beauty. New Agers see color as energy.

Anyone who deals with the supernatural will tell you that color is a language of the spirits. In the New Age movement color therapy, or chromotherapy, is very common. New Age color therapists claim that colors are able to help you by changing your moods, healing you, predicting your future, and can even give you power. Color therapy has been used by psychics to view auras. (New Agers believe that auras are patterns of colors that surround the body.) Theosophists use it as a method of spiritual diagnosis. Some say it originated with Egyptian sun worship. In his book *Child Spirit,* Dr. Samuel Silverstein claims that children can see spirits materialize by color particles.[1]

Here is an example of how New Agers take something that God has created and pervert its meaning. The rainbow that God created was to show Noah that He would never again destroy the world by a flood. But the rainbow, which was a blessing to Noah, is used by the New Age movement to symbolize the bridge into the occult; the bridge that crosses from the natural to the supernatural. Again, it becomes a part of worship. They worship the creation instead of the Creator.

Let me give one more illustration of this perversion. My son recently came back from a mission trip to Canada. All the young people were taught how to use the wordless book and the wordless bracelet. Each bead and every color opens a new avenue of witness, such as:

Black = represents sin
Red = represents the shed blood of Jesus
Green = represents growing in Christ
White = represents being washed clean by the blood of Christ
Gold = represents Heaven's splendor

This I believe is a great witnessing tool. The difference is that the colors in the wordless book and beads have no saving supernatural powers in and of themselves. The New Age movement claims they do.

Is it by accident that the Power Rangers are color coordinated, or is it by design? Some may be eager to point out that a man like David Benoit is just reaching to make claim that color coordination is something more than just for fashion in the Power Rangers case. Well, let's examine this theory using occult writings to prove a point. Are the colors an accident? I say, "Absolutely not!"

If you remember in the chapter entitled "Are the Power Rangers Morphing Your Children," I talked about how Jason Frank, the Green Ranger, was growing too old and the execs at Fox wanted to get rid of him. They found they couldn't kill him off. They had to "morph" him into another color. Now Jason Frank is the White Ranger.

In an article entitled "Power Rangers, Tommy Is Reborn" (*USA Today*, October 19, 1994), a statement is made that proves the colors are by divine design. "Fox execs insist there's deep symbolism behind making Tommy the White Ranger." What is this symbolism they talk about? To answer that question we must refer to occult literature.

> The Russian painter Valisy Kandinsky, one of the founders of the modern movement in art, believed that colors have a corresponding spiritual vibration and that color harmony must rest only on a corresponding vibration in the human soul.[2]

The Druids used colors in their religious system. Who are the Druids, you might ask. Let me introduce you to a group of people who for centuries have worked demonism as their religion. In his book *New Age Cults and Religions,* Texe Marrs relates a story of Julius Caesar's first encounter with this religious sect.

> When Julius Caesar conquered Britain in 60 A.D. he was astonished and shocked at the perverse and grotesque nature of the religious system practiced by the conquered peoples. He and his soldiers discovered blood-stained rows of trees; howling, black-clad priests; screaming and violent women. Later, Caesar himself wrote of seeing mass burning of human and animal victims in huge wicker cages. He told of the human sacrifices that were common to these pagans who worshipped the sun god, Hu, and the goddess Ceridwen.[3]

Many occultists believe that Jesus was taught how to perform miracles by these vile people. We totally reject that theory. Jesus is God. Something else that Texe brings out in his book that I found fascinating is that "the Druids held sway in Great Britain in the pre-Christian era. The mysterious circular network of stones in the ruins of Stonehenge are one of the few remains of this unholy religion, whose god Hu was symbolized by the serpent and his goddess by the egg."[4] What interested me about this quote is that the Power Rangers went to a sacred temple site in the Power Rangers movie to receive their powers. The site resembled Stonehenge, and Ivan the Ooze came out of a huge egg. So that we don't get too far off the subject of colors, let's look at how the Druids still use colors today as part of their religion.

The Druids use colors to identify their ranks. For example, green represents the bards (a singer of poetry in the Celtic religion). Blue represents those who are recent initiates, and the white robes represent the chief Druids. Don't you find it a little more than coincidental that Jason Frank, as the White Ranger, is the leader or chief of the group, and that they received their initiation of power at a Stonehenge replica site? Maybe we are starting to see the deep symbolism Fox execs were talking about.

The Aztecs spoke of four main colors: red, yellow, white, and black, which were also the four main types of corn, the four cardinal directions, and the gods associated with them. The Pueblo, Cherokee, and other Indian tribes also assign special colors and myth qualities to the four directions.[5]

Let's look at the colors of the Power Rangers:

O **Black Ranger.** Black is linked with night and darkness and, by extension, with death, the night that ends a man's day, with mourning and sorrow, with evil, the Devil, and the "powers of darkness." Black magic is evil magic; a black day is one of disaster; a black sheep is the one that goes astray.[6] I think you get the point of black.

O **White Ranger.** We already touched on white as representing the chief status of a Druid priest. White can also represent purity and holiness. Yet the Bible tells us that our righteousness is as filthy rags. The Bible tells us that there is none righteous, no not one. Yet, Jesus Christ was and is pure. He is the spotless Lamb of God that takes away the sins of the world.

O **Green Ranger.** Green represents earth and its life-giving qualities. Green is peaceful. Now we see Jason go from peaceful to powerful.

O **Red Ranger.** Red is preeminently the color of blood and the words for "red" in English, French, German, and Latin all stem from a root word which probably meant blood. But red also means bloodshed and is the color of the planet and war god Mars.[7] (When Satanists are practicing sexual magic they dress in red.)

O **Yellow Ranger.** Yellow is also ambivalent. As a color of the sun and gold, it means perfection, wealth, glory, and power. But yellow can also symbolize jealousy, hatred, cowardice, and treachery.[8]

O **Blue Ranger.** The symbolism of blue is also complicated. It is the color of the unclouded sky. It is linked with supreme gods ruling from the sky; it is the color of Jupiter.

O **Pink Ranger.** Pink could represent a feminine color.

The executive board at Fox said that there is a deep significant reason for changing the color of Jason Frank. Our goal in this article is not to discredit color, but to help us understand what this secret meaning is.

CASPER, THE UNHOLY GHOST

It's your typical love story. Ghost needs a friend. Girl needs a friend. Ghost sees girl on television. Ghost makes arrangements for them to get together. You know this kind of love story. It's a very familiar one. It's a story where the father is a single parent, the daughter needs someone to hold on to, and the ghost is just what she needs.

Well, if you're confused then you haven't seen the movie *Casper.* I will try to unfold the story for you without sounding like a movie critic. The first point that needs to be made is that Americans are suddenly obsessed with communicating with the dead. Why is this? And why are the movies directed toward such young viewers? *Ghost, The Lion King, Pocahontas,* and *Casper* all have the same theme: those who are dead can help us through our trials. No longer are children encouraged to seek God's help in times of trouble. All they need is a spirit to guide them. Any good teacher will tell you the best way to teach is by repetition. When children see how accessible these spirits are they have no fear in trying to contact them. Maybe that is the reason why the Ouija board is the number two best-selling game to children ages twelve through seventeen, and especially to girls in that age group.

The story line in *Casper* goes something like this. A

very evil woman named Carrigan Crittenden inherits a haunted castle from her father who has just died. She thinks there is treasure in the house so she tries to find it. Instead of finding treasure she finds Casper, the maybe-a-little-too-friendly ghost, and three other poltergeisting spirits that inhabit the estate. Casper begins to watch TV and sees Dr. Harvey being interviewed. Through psychology, this Dr. Harvey can help ghosts find the problems that hinder them from going into the next life. From the very beginning you know he's on the right track to contact spirits. He has a pentagram and other tools which any good occultist would need in order to make contact with the supernatural.

Well, Casper not only notices this doctor who can help ghosts, he also notices his very cute daughter named Kat. So immediately, Casper makes sure that Carrigan sees the broadcast. He knows that she would pay to have this ghost buster come in with his lovely daughter who needs a friend.

The first time Casper sees this girl, she is in his bed. He responds by saying, "There's a girl in my bed. Yes!!" It amazes me how Hollywood can make a bed available to an excited young person, even if that young person is dead. (Of course, we don't believe that Casper is a dead boy. He is a demon spirit.)

The sad part about it is that Casper finally does win the heart of the girl and the audience says, "Yes!!" Somehow it sounds a little strange that people would want to see a spirit and a girl become intimate friends. How does this happen? When you first meet the character who plays Casper, you are not at all intimidated by him. He is very likable and someone you would have no problem bonding with. The key word is "bonding." Bonding is very important in human development. Everyone has experienced rejection at some point in their life and we find it easy to relate to rejection. No one ever wants to be rejected but we do want to be accepted. So when Casper helps Kat out of her rejection, he automatically becomes noble in our eyes. How can anyone say anything bad about those, be they human or be they supernatural, who are considerate of the needs of others who suffer rejection. And that's my point—you have bonded with this character. Now when you hear someone who rejects Casper, as I do, you automatically come to his defense. But remember, Casper is not a human, he is a spirit.

The movie had a phrase in it that went something like this. Ghosts are spirits of people who have unfinished business on this planet. The Bible teaches that it is appointed unto man once to die and after this is the judgment. The rich man in Hell could not contact his brothers from the dead (Luke 16:19–31). Talking to the dead, or necromancing, is addressed in previous chapters, so I will not elaborate on this subject of the talking dead.

I have learned, through talking with people who have poltergeisting spirits in their homes, that bonding is a part of a demon's plan. Here are a couple of examples:

I was speaking one night in a church when I was approached by a young lady who proceeded to tell me this unbelievable story. She said, "Mr. Benoit, have you ever heard of people talking to ghosts?" This girl told me that her house was inhabited by a young Indian boy. She said that the first time she met him it scared her, but after awhile she realized that he was not going to harm her so she accepted him. According to her story, she believes her house was built over an Indian burial ground so that's why he is there. She claimed to have become quite friendly with the spirit that took the form of a little Indian boy. "Sometimes I have to get on him for running in the house," she told me.

Now if you think that story is strange, let me tell you more. The Lord is my witness, as well as a few church members who gathered around to hear this story. While this one young lady was telling me about her young Indian ghost, another girl jumped right into the conversation and said, "Is he about this tall?" She made a mark in the air about four feet high. "Yes!" the other girl replied. She continued, "Does he have long straight hair that comes down to here?" She pointed to shoulder length. "That's right," the first lady replied. The second lady said, "I have one that lives in my house, too!" When I left the conversation, these two women were still sitting in the pew comparing ghosts. The thing I found amazing was that after the initial scare, both of these women had befriended and bonded with these spirits.

In one of the movie scenes, Kat asked Casper if they could hurt one another. He assured her that they could not. The American Indians had a lot of dealings with demonic spirits through the worship of spirits like earth, wind, water, and fire. So it doesn't surprise me that these demon spirits will, many times, materialize as Indians.

Another Indian spirit story was told to me by a program director at a Christian television station in Florida. His Indian-impersonating spirit was an Indian chief. No, he didn't run through the house but he had a favorite chair in the living room. The man who told me this story said that after the initial scare, he, too, accepted this spirit as part of the family.

Do I believe these stories? Yes. It says in 1 Timothy 4:1: "Now the Spirit speaketh expressly, that in the latter times some shall depart from the faith, giving heed to seducing spirits, and doctrines of devils." The word *seducing* means to deceive by being crafty. The Greek words for "seducing spirits" can also imply sexual deception. That was the one thing that bothered me about Casper. He had a sexual attraction to this girl. That is the reason he said, "Yes!!" when he saw her in bed. Not only that, but he was jealous of a boy named Vic. In the movie, Casper is trying to talk Kat out of hanging around with Vic at her party. Casper says, "I'm a good dancer, and I don't need a costume [it was a Halloween party]. What's this guy got that I don't have?" "A pulse," said Kat, "and a tan."

Through the magic of Kat's mother, who is dead, Casper is allowed to become a boy again for a couple of hours. When he walks down the stairs of the mansion only one girl is sitting alone, rejected by all the human teens. Now Casper is there to be her friend and to save her from all those who have rejected her. It is not uncommon for people to seek the supernatural after being rejected by the natural.

At the end of the movie, Casper turns back into a ghost. All of the children and teachers run away, leaving behind a very happy ghost named Casper, a very satisfied girl named Kat, her father, and three ghost uncles who party the night away.

In closing, I might say that those who bond with spirits may be opening themselves up to bondage.

TURMOIL IN THE TEEPEE, OR WHO KIDNAPPED REBECCA?

I am amazed at the providence of God. Yesterday, I flew into Great Falls, Montana. Today, I preached in a mission church in the heart of the Blackfeet Indian Reservation. Tonight, I am writing this chapter on *Pocahontas*.

Sometimes it's hard to separate the "culture" of a people from the "religion" of a people, so there were a lot of questions as I spoke to the audience of this church. Many of their families' religious beliefs went hand-in-hand with the Wiccan belief. You must understand that the traditional religion of the Native American is pantheism and animism. Pantheism is, simply stated, "god is all and all is god." Willy Peterson, in his book *A New Age Primer*, defines animism as "a pagan view of nature that inanimate objects contain the spark of divine consciousness and are, therefore, worthy of our devotion; also, the practice of worshipping a superior intelligence within simple animate or inanimate objects. Example: Druid worship of oak trees."[1] Pocahontas had Grandmother Willow. As Christians, we do not worship the creation. Instead, we believe that God's creation is to show God's power in order to draw man to Himself.

Romans 1:20 says:

For the invisible things of him from the creation of the world are clearly seen, being understood by the things that are made, even his eternal power and Godhead; so that they are without excuse.

In Disney's version of *Pocahontas,* it shows her consulting with a 200-year-old willow tree. This was her spirit guide. Animism is introduced to Pocahontas when Grandmother Willow tells her to listen to the spirits. "All around you are spirits. They live in the earth, the water, the sky. If you listen they will guide you."

Later in the movie, Pocahontas introduces John Smith to animism, pantheism, and the evolution of animals to be equal with men. "You think of this land and everything in it as something you can claim. But we know everything here as a friend and as a brother. Come, run the forest trails with me, John! Stop trying to figure out what everything is worth. Swim in the crystal clear water with my brothers, the heron and the otter. See how high the trees grow? Don't just cut them down. Listen to the cry of the wolf. You cannot put a price on that." Then John Smith says to Pocahontas, "I'm beginning to see things your way."

So according to Disney, John Smith was the first English man to be converted to pantheism and animism. Later in the movie, Grandmother Willow speaks to John Smith personally because she thought he was a good soul, and he was handsome. It's amazing how easily Disney pulled the ultimate switch with John Smith and Pocahontas. According to history, John Smith was not converted to animism, but Pocahontas was converted to Christianity. If this movie was just for entertainment and not for indoctrination, then why did they give a positive light on New Age beliefs and a negative light on the Christian belief?

Disney has never portrayed Christianity in a positive light. Even on the main street in Disney's theme parks the church is deliberately omitted. Recently, Disney produced a movie called *Priest* that had Catholics up in arms. It portrayed one of the priests as a homosexual. The sad part about this is that Christians are the main contributors to Disney's revenues. For years, Christians have been duped into believing that Disney is a good, wholesome, Christian-based organization. Nothing could be further from the truth. If Disney, who now owns the ABC network, has any Christian and family values, then the first thing that will go is *NYPD Blue*. Don't count on it!!

It's a known fact that for years Disney has produced films that were not for children or Christians under their subsidiary, Touchstone Films. Some of Disney's films, like *Splash* and *Fantasia,* contain nudity. Yet people will say that's not Disney, that's Touchstone Films, but in reality it's the same company. Suppose you found out that Disney had a film company that produced X-rated movies. Would we tolerate that? According to the *Charlotte Observer,* September 5, 1995, a group called American Life League (ALL), "an organization opposed to abortion and claiming 300,000 supporters nationwide, has asked Disney officials to apologize to fans for including, what the group says, is inappropriate sexual material in several of its films." Some of the movies that have been cited by the American Life League are:

Aladdin—The phrase, "Good teenagers, take off your clothes" is supposedly found spoken subliminally in one scene.

The Lion King—According to this group, the word "sex" is spelled out in the leaves when Simba falls to the ground.

The Little Mermaid—In this film, the minister at Ariel's wedding is supposed to be sexually aroused. Disney claims it was the minister's knee.

"Last year, viewers of the laser disc version of Disney's *Who Framed Roger Rabbit* claimed that when they freeze-framed the animation, they found everything from frontal nudity to Michael Eisner's home phone number." Is this just a vicious attack on Disney? Obviously they have an answer for every allegation.

There are those who will side with Disney from the secular media, and there are those who will agree with the American Life League. Bill Melendez, a former award winner in the field of animation, was interviewed by *Entertainment Tonight* on September 9, 1995. He admitted that after reviewing the questionable scenes, it was quite obvious that the scenes in question were not only very clear, but well thought out.

Are these scenes in question real, or are they just a figment in the imagination of radical Christians? My answer to this is, so what?!!! If Christians do want to boycott Disney, boycott them because of their stand against our Christian values. Example—homosexuality, witchcraft, etc. I want to emphasize again, let's not be blinded by the subtle and miss the obvious (see introduction).

According to the *AFA Journal*, July 1995, the headline states, "Porn Photographer Directs New Disney Film."

> Disney/Miramax's *Kids* is the directorial debut of photographer Larry Clark. Clark, described as "a photographer of the adolescent demimonde," is featured in the current issue of *Gayme*, a pornographic magazine catering to pedophiles and featuring nude and semi-nude photographs of boys. Clark, who spent five years at an Oklahoma state penitentiary for assault with a deadly weapon, also focuses on teen suicide in his photographs.

You would think that, with all the power and prestige that Disney has, they could find a better director than a man with these credentials. Or is this the direction in which Disney is moving?

The *Daily Variety,* May 16, 1995, reports that Miramax Films, a wholly-owned Disney company, premiered its movie, *Lie Down With Dogs,* at the seventh annual New York Lesbian and Gay Film Festival in June. Not only is Disney involved with movies that endorse homosexuality, they have published a book through its subsidiary, Hyperion, entitled *Growing Up Gay: From Left Out to Coming Out.* The authors are identified as "funny gay males." Who would have thought that I would have to pick my words so carefully when talking about Disney so as not to offend the parents of children who are going to read this book.

If you think I'm getting overly excited about Disney's involvement with the homosexual movement, the following article may make a believer out of you.

> Walt Disney Co. will extend health benefits to domestic partners and children of homosexual workers next year, becoming one of the last major entertainment groups to do so. Disney spokesman John Dryer said the change does not apply to heterosexuals. He wouldn't comment on the policy's impact on Disney's image.[2]

Maybe, just maybe, Disney is becoming heterophobic.

Another aspect of the movie *Pocahontas* that I take offense to is that Disney would take one of America's first converts to Christianity and make her a New Age guru. Did you know that Pocahontas' baptism is part of a massive mural in the rotunda of the U.S. Capitol building? And did you know that after Pocahontas was baptized her name was changed to Rebecca, which means "devoted one"? That's the reason why this chapter is subtitled "Who Kidnapped Rebecca?"

Such a perversion of truth should not be tolerated by

Christians. Not only was there a distortion of spiritual truth, there was also a distortion of historic truth. People were very offended by Disney's historic incorrectness. Yet, if Disney were to do it again, people would say, "Well, that's not so bad." By the third movie, it would not even be an issue. By the fourth time, people would think other people who spoke out against it were radical. I know this to be true because Christians have been conditioned to accept demonic doctrine the same way. That is the reason they cry, "Historically incorrect!" and not, "Spiritually incorrect!"

At the time John Smith met Pocahontas she was about twelve years old. This is quite a different person from the Pocahontas that Disney portrayed in the movie. There is no historical evidence that Pocahontas was ever in love with John Smith.

Another misrepresentation: John Smith was not shot by Governor Ratcliffe. Suppose someone portrayed your great, great, great grandfather as a stark-raving, gold-blinded madman, as Disney did to Governor Ratcliff. How would you feel? We are not talking about a fairy tale character. We are talking about the character assassination of a real person. Changing history to be politically correct is not uncommon these days. History is being rewritten to accommodate the future.

The movie *Pocahontas* also spiritually misrepresented the American Indian. After spending several days with the Blackfeet tribe, I realized that most Indians today do not adhere to the occult belief of animism. There are many godly Indians who love Jesus Christ. You may say that in the days of Pocahontas all Indians believed in animism. That is no more the truth than it is to say that because England claimed to be a Christian country, everyone in England was a Christian. As I said earlier, God, even through His creation, could lead people to worship Him as the one true God (Rom. 1:20).

Obviously, spending three days with the Blackfeet Indians doesn't make me an expert on tribal customs, but it did help me to understand that we should not stereotype or label people. I did not see one Indian living in a teepee. They live in wood-framed houses just like you and I. I did not see one Indian wearing moccasins. Many of them wore Reeboks and Nikes. I did not see one Indian riding bareback on a wild horse. Many drive four-wheel, all-terrain vehicles. I didn't see one Indian wearing only a loin cloth with a bow and arrow around his neck. I saw people wearing Charlotte Hornets caps, Chicago Bulls tee-shirts, and San Antonio Spurs jackets.

What am I trying to say? When we hear the word "Indian," most of us have a wrong impression and see a Hollywood image of the Indian culture. And again, when people think of the Native American religion, they have a Hollywood version of earth worship. I am here to say that the church building was filled with people singing songs about Jesus. The altars were filled with people praying for family members who need to be saved. Eyes were filled with tears as a family sang "Beulah Land." Don't let Hollywood stereotype the Native American as an unlearned, heathen culture. The great missionary David Brainard died ministering to the American Indians he so dearly loved.

Disney uses three forms of divination in the movie *Pocahontas:*

1. Dreams. Throughout the whole movie, Pocahontas was searching for her interpretation of a dream she had of a spinning arrow. Near the end of the movie she finds that the spinning arrow was John Smith's compass.

Believe it or not, libraries are putting more books on their shelves dealing with dreams. There are seventy-nine books on dreams in my public library alone. New Agers are about to start a dream network just like the psychic network. New Agers will quickly tell you God wants to show you your future through dreams.

Did God use dreams in Daniel's and Joseph's lives? The answer is yes. God knew this question would come up so he answered it in Deuteronomy 13:1–3:

> If there arise among you a prophet, or a dreamer of dreams, and giveth thee a sign or a wonder, And the sign or the wonder come to pass, whereof he spake unto thee, saying, Let us go after other gods, which thou hast not known, and let us serve them; Thou shalt not hearken unto the words of that prophet, or that dreamer of dreams: for the LORD your God proveth you, to know whether ye love the LORD your God with all your heart and with all your soul.

Will New Agers lead you to God through Jesus Christ, His Son? I don't think so.

2. Fortune-telling. Divination was used by the medicine man to foretell the coming of the white man. During my first day on the reservation, the pastor and I were driving down a dirt road. He pointed out a frame built with small trees and branches. He told me this was called a sweat lodge. A sweat lodge is a place where some of the Indian men go to practice spiritism. The wooden frame would be covered by animal skins. Then they would heat the rocks red hot and add water to the stones, creating steam. It is in this hut that men would hear demonic voices and feel a demonic presence. Disney called it the longhouse but the Blackfeet would call it the sweat lodge.

3. Astrology. Grandmother Willow said to Pocahontas, "Spirits live in the earth, the water, the sky." Pocahontas was told that the spirits would guide her if she would listen with her heart. The problem with the heart is that it is "deceitful" and "desperately wicked: who can know it?" (Jer. 17:9). Out of the heart proceeds murder and other evil thoughts. We have already discussed animism and pantheism, dealing with worship of the earth. Here Grandmother Willow tells Pocahontas to follow the spirits of the sky, the heavenly body. In *The Lion King,* Simba's father told him that the stars were ascended masters who would help him. The Bible condemns astrology.

> Thou art wearied in the multitude of thy counsels. Let now the astrologers, the stargazers, the monthly prognosticators, stand up, and save thee from these things that shall come upon thee. Behold, they shall be as stubble; the fire shall burn them; they shall not deliver themselves from the power of the flame: there shall not be a coal to warm at, nor fire to sit before it (Isa. 47:13–14).

As a parent, you need to be very careful that Disney does not pull the same switch on your children that they pulled on Pocahontas in the movie by turning them from the Christian faith to animism and pantheism. Hopefully your children will not say what John Smith said to Pocahontas in the movie: "I'm beginning to see things your way."

INDIANS COMING OUT
OF THE CLOSET

Have you ever had the feeling that you were being duped but you didn't know how? This is how I felt when I saw *Indian In the Cupboard.*

When I see a movie with a child actor in it, the child is usually very streetwise and rebellious. So when I saw a 9-year-old boy who was obedient to his parents, who had no romantic scenes with a little girl, was not smarter than the teacher, had no clue as to how to work a computer, and had no bad language coming out of his mouth, I was completely thrown off guard. This kid was innocent. He wasn't even a master in martial arts. Throughout the movie, all the things that usually jump out at me were not there. Again, I knew I was being duped but I didn't know how. I walked out of the theater almost numb.

It kind of reminds me of a joke I heard some time ago about Indians. Legend has it that Indians used to be able to put their ears to the ground and hear things far away. One time this cowboy comes up to this old Indian man who had his ear to the ground. The Indian says to the cowboy, "Two wagons, one mule, twenty foot-soldiers, and three horses." The cowboy said to the old Indian, "Can you hear all that just by putting your ear to the ground?" "No," the Indian replied, "that's what ran over me yesterday!"

That's how it was with me during this movie. My ears were fixed on every word, my eyes were locked in on each image in the movie, and I still felt like I had been walked over but didn't know how. It took me several days of rehashing these thoughts to come up with just how people are being programmed by this movie.

What About Magic?

There was a time when I could have said to the general reader that magic was bad and they would have all agreed. Now that people have been bombarded by that term, they say, "What's wrong with magic?"

Today Christians even let their children play a game called "Magic, the Gathering," which is nothing more than "Dungeons & Dragons" put into a card game. I'm sure that even some church youth groups play this game at activities. It's filled with spells, demons, sorcerers, and occultism, yet people in Christian circles see nothing wrong with it. I don't want to get sidetracked at this point. I'm just trying to say that forty years ago a game called "Magic" would never have been considered by the general Christian community. Now it is. We are being programmed. Have you been programmed?

Here's a good test: Are you saying at this point, "This man is really looking for something. Magic is just make-believe"? Magic is not just make-believe. It is an act of a person to manipulate the natural by using the supernatural. Real magic is not an illusion. It is an act performed by demonic forces.

The word *magician* is used at least fifteen times in the Old Testament. The main purpose of magicians was to keep people from trusting God. The best example of this can be found in Exodus 7:8–12:

> And the LORD spake unto Moses and unto Aaron, say-
> ing, When Pharaoh shall speak unto you, saying, Shew a
> miracle for you: then thou shalt say unto Aaron, Take
> thy rod, and cast it before Pharaoh, and it shall become a
> serpent. And Moses and Aaron went in unto Pharaoh,
> and they did so as the LORD had commanded: and Aaron
> cast down his rod before Pharaoh, and before his ser-
> vants, and it became a serpent. Then Pharaoh also called
> the wise men and the sorcerers: now the magicians of
> Egypt, they also did in like manner with their enchant-
> ments. For they cast down every man his rod, and they
> became serpents: but Aaron's rod swallowed up their rods.

Forty years ago, people accepted this passage as the
Word of God. They would have believed this story. Now it
is a fable. They have seen the special effects of Hollywood
perform this feat with the greatest of ease. Some no longer
believe the Bible to be literal. They doubt its validity, or
try to explain it away as a parable. Satan's ultimate goal is
to get people to doubt God's Word. His plan has been ac-
complished if you are reading this and saying, "This guy is
off the wall to believe people can really turn rods into ser-
pents." If you have been angered by this material, you are
right on target. Let's read the response of Pharaoh after
seeing this event take place. "And he hardened Pharaoh's
heart, that he hearkened not unto them; as the LORD had
said" (Exod. 7:13).

Instead of Pharaoh's heart melting at the sight of God's
power, he became hard and intolerant. Remember, the sun
that melts the butter is the same sun that hardens the
bricks. Every time the magicians countered God's miracles,
the heart of Pharaoh became harder.

It was this story in the Bible that helped me understand how I was duped by the movie *Indian In the Cupboard*. The young boy in the movie had been given a magic

cupboard. When wooden objects were put inside and the magic key was turned, the figures in the cupboard came to life. The boy first puts a wooden image of an Indian inside the cupboard, locks it, and then opens it to find that the figure has life.

Throughout the entire movie, whenever the boy needs something to help his new Indian friend, he brings it to reality by putting it into his magic cupboard and it comes to life. The characters who came to life were living lives in another reality. Without getting into a long dissertation, I'll simply say that New Age occultists believe that all things have life. That is why they pray to statues and idols. They believe that they actually hear and understand their prayers. The final point I want to make is that according to the book of Revelation, this giving of life to an image will be performed by the Beast in Revelation 13:13–15:

> And he doeth great wonders, so that he maketh fire come down from heaven on the earth in the sight of men, And deceiveth them that dwell on the earth by the means of those miracles which he had power to do in the sight of the beast; saying to them that dwell on the earth, that they should make an image to the beast, which had the wound by a sword, and did live. And he had power to give life unto the image of the beast, that the image of the beast should both speak, and cause that as many as would not worship the image of the beast should be killed.

Not only did the boy in the movie *Indian In the Cupboard* give life to these wooden figures, the spirits in *Mighty Morphin Power Rangers, the Movie* caused carved images of stone to have life which the Power Rangers had to fight. Michael Jackson did it in one of his videos. It is becoming very popular with special-effects people in Hollywood to give life to images that are made of wood and stone.

The second problem I had with this movie was the secrecy he had to maintain before his parents and teacher. Throughout the movie you had the feeling that if adults ever found out about this tremendous secret, something bad would happen. It's just another ploy to teach children not to trust adults. In a time when children need, more than ever before, to confide in their parents about what is happening in their lives, Hollywood teaches children that something bad will happen if adults find out what's going on in the child's life. Satan has always wanted to separate your child from you as a parent. He has always tried to cause doubt in the security of parental guidance. A child's most needed friend is a parent. Today, psychologists will admit that parents and children must communicate. Again, Satan is subtly trying to put enmity between parents and children.

The Bible tells us in Romans 1 that there will be no natural affection in reprobate homes. "Without natural affection" means there is no natural love for the family. You must understand that love and trust go together. How can children love their parents when they are constantly told they cannot trust them?

The very first thing Satan did in the garden was to get Eve to doubt her heavenly Father. She did, and that is why we are in our present sinful state.

TV—"TRANSFORMING VALUES"

The letters *TV* may stand for "transforming values" these days. Although I do not believe that the executives of the major television networks get together to formulate a plan to pervert our children, I do believe that they have views that are contrary to the Word of God, and they do not hesitate to share those views with your children.

The area which most TV entertainment shows deal with is primarily "value laden," i.e. promoting moral conduct of one sort or another. Traditional Judeo-Christian values versus secular, irreligious values. Promiscuity versus chastity, adultery versus fidelity. Dishonesty (making a fast buck, lying, etc.) versus honesty and integrity. True love and commitment versus lust and self-indulgence. Responsibility versus total freedom. Respect for human life versus violence. Respect for women versus exploitation.[1]

Our children are constantly bombarded with images of alternate lifestyles as the normal lifestyle. Some time ago, a team of university social scientists, Linda Lichter, Stanley Rothman, and Robert Lichter, published a 300-page study on the media elite. Their study was very revealing.

The television elite's social liberalism is also evidenced by their views on sex and morality, another focal point for television's critics. On such issues as abortion, homosexual rights, and extramarital sex, their views diverge sharply from traditional values. Ninety-seven percent believe that a woman has the right to decide for herself whether to have an abortion; even more striking, 91 percent agree strongly with this position. Four out of five do not regard homosexual relations as wrong. Only 5 percent feel strongly that homosexuality is wrong, compared to 49 percent who disagree strongly. An even greater proportion, 86 percent, support the rights of homosexuals to teach in public schools. Finally, a majority of those who feel strongly about this issue take a permissive stance; only 17 percent strongly agree that extramarital affairs are wrong. From this evidence, it would be difficult to over-estimate the clash of values when television's creative community confronts fundamental Christian critics like the Moral Majority or the Coalition for Better Television.[2]

It has been estimated that:

○ **The average child in America will watch approximately 18,000 hours of television by the time he/she graduates from high school.** I speak at Christian educators' conventions around the country and I always tell them that we, as Christian teachers, can teach children math, science, and English in school, but if the Devil is teaching them his values in the home through television and rock music, we will lose them. And Christian students are not exempt from these statistics.

○ **The average child in America will listen to approximately 12,500 hours of rock music by the time he/she graduates.** Television and rock music are two powerful media tools that are reaching the hearts of our children.

○ **Children will witness 13,000 killings on TV.** The question now is, "Does television affect the way they see death?" Does it instill in children the idea that it's okay to kill? Let's look at some statistics.

These are some excerpts from an article by Deborah Sharp, a writer for *USA Today:*

● A 9-year-old and her little brother left alone by their parents quarrel over a Nintendo game. The girl finds the family gun and blasts a hollow-point bullet into the 3-year-old's head.[3]

● The New York parents of a 5-year-old are facing three felony charges, including reckless endangerment, after the boy shot his 13-month-old half-sister in the head with a gun he thought was a toy.[4]

● The Lake Worth, Florida, father of an 11-year-old who took his dad's gun from a night stand and accidentally killed his 8-year-old brother, has been charged under the state's gun access law.[5]

Deborah Sharp was not citing these examples to show the violence of children, but to point out why the parents should be held responsible for the deaths that these children caused with the parents' guns. This is another attempt by the humanists to disarm Americans (and God forbid that we call them communist socialists lest we be politically incorrect!).

According to the FBI Uniform Crime Reports, the number of young killers under the age of fourteen is rising:

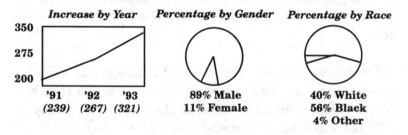

Increase by Year	Percentage by Gender	Percentage by Race
350		
275		
200		
'91 '92 '93	89% Male	40% White
(239) (267) (321)	11% Female	56% Black
		4% Other

The problem is not guns. We have had guns to protect homes since the colonial days. Why, then, are America's babies suddenly becoming murderers? Could it be that these children are being influenced by the medium of television? Before TV, people slept with their doors unlocked. Now there are bars on the windows of private homes!

Children are killing their parents and parents are killing their babies. God help us! If you are concerned about the violent tendencies in your child, and you have a gun and a TV, you might want get rid of one of them.

Recommended Reading from the Book Shelf

Fourteen Things Witches Hope Parents Never Find Out, David Benoit

The Devil's Disciples, Jeff Godwin

The Responsible Parent's Guide to TV, Colonel V. Doner

From Rock to Rock, Eric Burger

Turmoil In the Toy Box, Phil Phillips

Playing With Fire, John Weldon, James Bjornstad

Devil Take the Youngest, Winkie Pratney

Section II

EDUCATION BY THE HUMANISTS

CHILDREN
LIVING IN A HOSTILE WORLD

With MTV's constant images of violence, and while rock bands continually harp on themes of sex, violence, and suicide, children are being plunged headlong into a turbulant, hostile world. The undertow of these waves of violence, produced by the media elite, are quickly pulling these children from the safety of loving arms.

The six major problems youth deal with today are:

1. Gang violence
2. Domestic violence
3. Alcoholism and drugs
4. Teen pregnancies
5. Suicide
6. Education

○ **Gang Violence.** So you live in a nice, four-bedroom home in a pleasant, quiet development and the inner-city seems a million miles away. Then you turn on the news and story after story comes across your TV set about kids killing kids, drug wars, and inner-city rivals.

You must understand that there is a war going on and

it's not being fought on foreign soil. This one deals with ethnic cleansing, power, hatred, and acceptance. I was watching a program one day concerning young people talking about their need to be a part of the gang. Some girls wanted so badly to be accepted that they had sex with members of the gang whom they knew for a fact had AIDS.

Life in the inner-city has become a near death experience. Young people get a buzz living near the edge of death. Many gangs are well organized. They even have ranks just like the military. These inner-city rivals think nothing about raiding one another's area, or turf. Gangs can be divided many different ways: by location, like the south side kids; or by nationality, white, black, Hispanic, Chinese, etc.

Youth today, just like Hitler's youth, are taught that death is not an obstacle to avoid.

> The ideological training Hitler decreed was to bring up that unspoiled generation which will consciously find its way back to primitive instinct. Fairy tales were saturated with struggle and race as a childhood means of education to a heroic view of the world and of life. One volume was entitled *People Fight*. The Robinson Crusoe age groups were taught, from an early age, youth must be able to face a time when it may be ordered not merely to act, but also die.[1]

I praise the Lord for ministries that work with these kids. These ministries to the inner-city are like the spiritual Red Cross, delivering the bread of life and the living water to a dying people.

One such ministry I visited was an inner-city church in Philadelphia, the City of Brotherly Love. I was told of church members' cars being stolen off the street in front of the church during church services, and many acts of violence. One interesting story developed when the church bought a new front door for their building. This gang spray-painted it and ran off. One of the boys (these are only young children) felt bad because he had painted the church door so he returned during the service, stood in the back of the church, and asked the pastor if he could say something. The pastor granted him his request, and the young boy asked the church to forgive him. The pastor then invited the lad to come forward. He asked him if he knew where he would spend eternity if he were to die. To the pastor's amazement, the boy responded, "I'd go to Heaven!" The pastor proceeded to ask him why he thought he'd go to Heaven. The boy replied, "Because I cleaned off the door." What a sad commentary, when children do not know the Door to eternal life, Jesus Christ.

O **Domestic Violence.** Home is a place of rest; it's a shelter where children can find love and security, right? Wrong!

> Every 60 seconds in the U.S., a child is abused. More than 50,000 a year. The actual total may be much higher because many incidents go unreported. Estimates run between 1 million and 4 million children being mistreated in some way by adults. Two thousand children are killed each year by their own parents. The average age of the abusing mother is 26 years old; and the father, 30 years old. Alcohol plays a role in more than 60 percent of the cases.
>
> Frustrated parents (many of them teenagers themselves) have beaten infants whose only offense was crying or fussing from colic.[2]

The home has become a war zone for children. To add to the problems, young mothers bring boyfriends home with them, only to have them beat their children. The Ramones, a rock group, sing a song, "Beat the brat, beat the brat, beat the brat with a baseball bat."

Sometime ago, a mother took her three children on a lonely road and shot them while listening to a song by Duran Duran entitled "Hungry Like a Wolf." The song talks about not letting anything stand between love. Why did this woman shoot her children? Her boyfriend wouldn't marry her because she had them.

What about Susan Smith, the mother in South Carolina, who claimed someone kidnapped her two little boys, only to confess later that she had strapped them in the back seat of her car, pushed the car into the lake, and drowned her children.

Children are afraid to go home. Maybe that is the reason we have 50,000 children disappearing every year from homes. Listen to this story and weep.

> After a fire, a 9-year-old boy was found locked in his mother's basement. He had been there eight or nine months. He had only been allowed out once, on his birthday. Her live-in boyfriend did not like the child and threatened to leave her if she let him out. The boy's only companion was a parakeet, which had died in the fire. After the child was discovered, the authorities asked the mother how she could ignore her 9-year-old son for such a long time, and if, during his imprisonment, she ever heard him crying, asking for help, or making any sounds whatsoever? I'd just hear him singing to himself sometimes, she said.[3]

Physical abuse, mental abuse, and sexual abuse are not only confined to homes of drunkards. Christian homes are also affected by this evil lifestyle. Some time ago, I sat down and talked with a former artist who worked for Walt Disney. This man is a tremendous cartoonist. He grew up in a religious home. On the outside, his father was a well-respected, moral man who loved God. But in the home, this man would molest his son and then send the boy down into the basement, throw the Bible next to him, tell him to read it and repent of his sin. This was over forty years ago, and the man still hated his father so badly. I believe that if he had met him on the street he would have killed him. This is not the only case I have heard of where people claim to know God and yet still abuse their children.

Here is the sad part. Night after night, I see young people come to my services. They hate their parents because they won't let them stay out late to do drugs, or listen to rock music. They have never been beaten, they have never had to experience sexual abuse, they have never come home to find their mother beaten by their father, and they have never had to stay out late until the drunken parents would fall asleep. God help you, young person. There are millions of children who would trade places with you in a heartbeat. You ought to thank God every day for the parents you have. It's a sad day when godly parents are verbally abused by their children whom they have never abused. Your parents are not perfect people, but they are a far cry from the ones I described in this chapter.

○ **Alcohol and Tobacco.** Isn't it amazing how the government has declared war on the tobacco industry? The statistics are now out on how many children are smoking. News programs, talk shows, and other media are talking about smoking and it's damaging effects. We now have smoke-free work areas. We have non-smoking airline flights. Just this afternoon I went to a restaurant and the waitress asked me my seating preference: smoking or non-smoking. I replied, "To tell you the truth, I can't afford to eat out and smoke. Have you seen the price of cigarettes lately?"

I might be suffering from a false memory syndrome,

but it seems to me that a short time ago, the same politicians were talking about the benefits of legalizing marijuana. Now, if that isn't hypocritical, what is? Please don't misunderstand me. I am not going to fight for the rights of smokers. As a matter of fact, I have asthma and cannot tolerate cigarette smoke. My point is, our government is declaring all-out war on tobacco, and yet nothing is said about alcohol. Personally, I do not know of one person who has died of secondary smoke, yet every year over 50,000 people die on highways because of alcohol. If 50,000 are killed each year in alcohol-related accidents, how many more accidents are there that have no fatalities, but cause some kind of injury?

Alcohol has a long, complicated history in this country and unlike drugs, the American people accept alcohol. They have no interest in going back to Prohibition, but advocates of legalization should at least admit that legalized alcohol, which is responsible for some 100,000 deaths a year, is hardly a model for drug policy.[4]

Here are some astounding statistics given by the *Chicago Tribune* in 1984. Alcohol is blamed in:

64% of all murders	34% of all rapes
60% of all child abuse	30% of all suicides
53% of all fire deaths	45% of all drownings
55% of all arrests nationally	50% of all traffic deaths
37% of all admissions to state and county mental hospitals[5]	

Anyone who thinks alcohol is a benign drink should remember the drunk driver from Carroll County, Kentucky, who slammed his pickup truck into a church bus killing 27 people. It's time we admit that America would be a lot better off today if Prohibition had worked.[6]

Most people don't know that I came from a broken home. My Dad was an alcoholic. I saw first-hand how alcohol and tobacco could destroy a life as well as a family. When my Dad would drink he changed from a meek, loving man into an angry, hateful man. He would get drunk in bars and then go home with other women. He would come home and fight with my mother. I don't need to tell you about alcohol because alcohol affects every family directly or indirectly. Today my father is a Christian. He accepted Jesus Christ as his personal Savior. Even though my Dad has only one lung (tobacco destroyed the other one) and you look at how years of using alcohol has destroyed him physically, my father can now sing, "Amazing grace, how sweet the sound, that saved a wretch like me!"

My two brothers have been in the penitentiary three times each. My uncle has been admitted to Angola State Penitentiary three times. I was in reform school by the time I was fifteen years old for possession of LSD blotter acid. I jokingly tell people, "My family lived a very sheltered life. We were all locked up!" I was golfing with a gentleman one day and he said, "Benoit, Benoit. What does that mean in French?" I told him it meant two to five years, depending on what you did when I was growing up!

Recently, America said good-bye to a sports legend. His name was Mickey Mantle. Mickey Mantle died because of years of alcohol and tobacco abuse. Former Surgeon General C. Everett Koop reported that over 300,000 people have died because of tobacco, and over 100,000 people have died because of alcohol. I guess you could call it legalized killing!

FLEECING THE LAMBS

So, your children come from a Christian home and they go to a Christian school. Surely, they must be safe. I wish I could comfort you by saying that this is true, but I can't. A 1994 survey taken by the Barna Research Group of 3,700 young people proved differently. Josh McDowell, in his book, *Right From Wrong*, reveals some of their findings and it is alarming.

The participants are youth who are intensely involved in church activities (Sunday school, worship, youth group, Bible study), and who overwhelmingly identify their parents as loving, and their family experience as positive.

● Two out of every three (66 percent) of our kids (ages

eleven to eighteen) lied to a parent, teacher, or other adults.
- Six in ten (59 percent) lied to their peers.
- Nearly half (45 percent) watched MTV at least once a week.
- One in three (36 percent) cheated on an exam.
- Nearly one in four (23 percent) smoked a cigarette or used another tobacco product.
- One in five (20 percent) tried to physically hurt someone.
- One in nine (12 percent) had gotten drunk.
- Nearly one in ten (8 percent) had used illegal, non-prescription drugs.[1]

The same survey showed that by the time these Christian school students turned eighteen years of age the statistics didn't get better.

- 55 percent had sexual contact with the opposite sex.
- 50 percent say they are stressed out.
- 55 percent say they are confused.
- 74 percent say they are looking for answers.[2]

Somehow the enemy is getting in. Apparently, there is an open door somewhere, and before parents find it their tender, loving lamb is fleeced. If these are the Christian young people, can you imagine the turmoil that is raging in those children without the Christian influence at home and in school?

For the last fifteen years, I have had the privilege of speaking at hundreds of Christian schools, and ministering to thousands of Christian school students. I am invited every year to present seminars to Christian educators about youth problems. The first statement I make is, "I believe in Christian education, but the Devil home schools." We can teach children math, science, even the Bible, but if they are learning their values from rock musicians on MTV, or from television programs or movies, they will grow up confused about Christian values. If life is a beach, someone ought to put up a sign, "Beware of Undertows!"

While attending college in Lynchburg, Virginia, I lived on an island right in the middle of the James River. Some people have lost their lives in this river because it is very deceptive. On the surface it seems to be reasonably calm, but under the surface was a raging current.

There have been millions of young Christians throughout the ages who thought they could wade in the pool of life, only to be dragged under by the undercurrent produced by godless friends and an evil society. The stealing of the young is not something new to the Devil's crowd. Hitler said, "Those who have the youth, have the future." Hitler's plan was not hampered by the Christian influence.

> For most young people, there was little resistance. The enthusiasm for the Fuhrer canceled out all other interests. Even when church groups or parents pleaded with children to keep away from Hitler's youth, their hearts and souls had been captured by the uniforms, the fife and drums, and the example of their peers, so that not to be included in the Fuhrer's glorious movement became the worst kind of punishment.[3]

There were three things that lured the children (including Christians) away from the loving arms of caring parents:

1. Fashion. When the children saw those nice, neatly pressed uniforms compared to their tattered clothes, they had to have them. Is fashion important to your child? If everyone is wearing baggy clothes, do they have to have it?

If everyone at school has to have certain kinds of jeans, is that a must for your child? If everyone is wearing the most expensive tennis shoes in the store, do your children rant and rave until they have them? Wearing "in" things is not wrong. Fashion becomes dangerous if children can't live without it. This is a subtle way of programming children to follow the masses.

2. Music. This was the second wave of influence among these children. When the fife and drum corp came marching down the street, children could hear them and lined the streets. Just like when we were young and heard the music from the ice cream truck, we begged our parents for a dime or quarter and took off following the music. Even though following the ice cream truck is harmless, I wish I could say the same about the music children are following today. The Pied Piper is pushing death music, sex music, rebellious and anti-Christian music, and the children are marching faithfully to it. The use of music as a call to worship is not a new thing. We read in Daniel 3:4–6 about some young men who basically had to "face the music."

> Then an herald cried aloud, To you it is commanded, O people, nations, and languages, That at what time ye hear the sound of the cornet, flute, harp, sackbut, psaltery, dulcimer, and all kinds of musick, ye fall down and worship the golden image that Nebuchadnezzar the king hath set up: And whoso falleth not down and worshippeth shall the same hour be cast into the midst of a burning fiery furnace.

These three young men had convictions, and were willing to take a stand for what they believed. My prayer for you is that your children will be able to stand when the music is played.

3. Peer pressure. "Why can't I? Everybody else is doing it!" If these words echo through your house, there is some need to be concerned. Many times after addressing an audience, people will come up to me with concerns about controlling their children. They say, "Mr. Benoit, if I tell my 5-year-old he can't have some toy, he will throw a fit!" At this I respond, "If you cannot control your child at five years old, wait until he is fifteen years old!"

You must understand that someone is changing the value system of your child. To recapture that value system may not be easy.

As I talk to young people about friends, I use the story of Samson. Samson's mother and father were godly people. Most people do not realize that even Samson's birth was announced by an angel (see Judges 13:3.) We all know how Samson died, blinded by the Philistines. There were three important keys to the downfall of Samson:

1. **He told his parents what to do instead of being obedient to them.** "And he came up, and told his father and his mother, and said, I have seen a woman in Timnath of the daughters of the Philistines: now therefore get her for me to wife" (Judg. 14:2).

2. **Samson looked to the world to supply him a wife.**

3. **Samson looked toward the Devil's crowd to supply him with friendship.** "And it came to pass, when they saw him, that they brought thirty companions to be with him" (Judg. 14:11). Young people outside of the will of God generally do not pick their friends. The Devil will appoint them.

If you are a young person reading this portion of the book and you have said to your parents, who are concerned about your friends, "These are my friends, and I'm old enough to pick my own friends," more than likely they are appointed. If your friends really exemplify the love of God, your parents would have no question. If your friends are a part of the worldly crowd, your parents should be concerned. If you were a parent, you would be concerned if you loved the Lord and your child's friends didn't.

Let me close this chapter with a story I heard about a fairly intelligent fly. One day this fly was flying by a spider web. It was all nice and neat, and the spider encouraged the fly to come in and sit down for a while. "You must be exhausted," said the spider. "Come in and have a little tea and rest." Well, this fairly intelligent fly responded, "What! Do I look stupid? There are no other flies in your house. If I fly into your house, you will snatch me and eat me. You see, I'm a fairly intelligent fly." As the fly flew away, he saw a whole group of flies. They were dancing around, seeming to be having a great time. He flew right down to be with the group of other flies. As soon as his feet hit the surface, he realized it was sticky and he could not get off the ground. Then, and only then, did he realize that it was fly paper. You see, he was a fairly intelligent fly.

Many young people have thought they were safe because others were doing it, only to find that it was a trap set by the Devil!

WHO BENEFITS FROM ILLITERACY?

An Interview with Susan Forsyth

For several years, Susan Forsyth has done legislative work for Concerned Women for America. While living in South Carolina she became involved in research of the educational system and discovered some startling evidence. Her state was deeply entrenched in Outcome Based Education (OBE). More unusual was the fact that the state and those in the educational hierarchy denied its existence, and that's when things got interesting!

David: Susan, tell us about your experience in South Carolina.

Susan: I was verbally attacked for being involved in the education "battle" in Greenville County. They said, "You have no children in the public school system." This was an interesting twist. I am a taxpayer and a substantial amount of my real estate and sales tax dollars go toward education in my state. I am also concerned with what has happened to education as a whole. Thirdly, many of the public school programs tend to spill over into the private school sector and I basically wanted to "nip it in the bud" before every school was infested with the OBE philosophy! For them to use that excuse is quite silly. After all, according to *Forbes* magazine, 22 percent of the teachers who belong to the NEA (National Education Association) send their children to private schools. Bill Clinton does, too![1]

One thing the educationalists will try to do to you when you "disagree" with their programs is to label you a "fundamentalist-right-wing-Christian-conservative" whose goal is to put "religion" into the schools. Interestingly, a few of the parents I was involved with were far from being "Christian right-wing fanatics"!

Another goal is to discredit you in any manner. For example, I was on WGGS in South Carolina discussing OBE, what to look for in your school, and evidence of Outcome Based Education in South Carolina. Less than twelve hours after the show was aired, the Greenville County school board had a meeting and a video of the show was played. An outline was passed out with a rebuttal to the points I had made on the show! These liberals were so scared of being uncovered they spent taxpayer money trying to "disprove" me. The education establishment cannot stand on their own two feet and praise their own programs for what they are doing, so they purposely attack anyone who brings attention to them. They create a "crisis" and can justify their paranoia.

South Carolina is of national importance in "bashing-the-right." Educational seminars were sponsored where conservative and Christian groups were discussed, as well as parents involved in opposition to the education movement. Isn't this strange? Shouldn't they be discussing educational matters instead of people, parents, and groups?

The NBC affiliate in Greenville was denied access to one of their seminars, which makes you wonder what they were really trying to hide behind those closed doors!

Another sleazy tactic they are using is in "letters to the editor." Severe religious-right bashing occurs with encouragement from a group called VOICE (Voters Organized In Children's Education), an ultra-far-left organization. My point is this: if these liberals are successful in bashing the conservative Christian voice in South Carolina, they will use these tactics elsewhere, attempting to create a place for themselves. After all, the liberals think they are "mainstream America"! Please be aware of these tactics and do know that you are not alone when you're in the midst of this battle.

David: Is our educational system working?

Susan: Well, the statistics are morbid. Over 72 million adults are functionally illiterate. They can't read or write above a fifth-grade level.[2] We spend over $225 billion in trying to fix it, too.[3]

David: Some people may argue that if there were more finances, there would be higher academic performance.

Susan: Twenty years ago we spent $51.7 billion on education. In 1992 we spent a whopping $253.4 billion. This was a 390 percent increase.[4]

So let's look at SAT (Standard Achievement Test) scores. In 1972, only 74,000 students scored in the 200-299 range for verbal portions. In 1991, over 134,000 students scored in that bottom range.[5] Let's look at the states that have the highest SAT scores and how much they spend per pupil. Iowa has the highest scores and ranks twenty-seventh in spending. North and South Dakota are second and third, ranging forty-fourth and forty-second in pupil spending. Utah is fourth in highest scores, yet they rank at the bottom of spending at number fifty-one. Minnesota has the fifth highest scores and ranks twenty-fifth in spending.[6] Obviously there is no direct correlation between increased spending and increased student achievement. Per pupil spending has increased 441 percent over the past twenty years, too, yet students are not performing.

What about the ACT test? Students' grade point averages have been rising steadily over the past twenty years. However, their ACT scores have been plummeting![7] This does not make sense. A study revealed that 75 percent of public school systems rated their graduates as academically prepared in the basic academic skills needed for employment.[8] But the president of the American Federation of Teachers says that 95 percent of the kids who go to college in the U.S. would not be admitted to colleges anywhere else in the world.[9] Why? Well, the typical eighth grader spends twenty-one and a half hours watching TV each week, does only five and a half hours of homework, and only two hours of reading.[10] Add to this the fact that classroom instructional time has dropped to twenty-two hours per week. Then kick in this fact: academics are slipping. Examples are classes called citizenship, life skills, environmentalism, career-ed, humanitarian activities, self-esteem programs, family living, higher order thinking skills, extensive art and music sessions. Our focus has shifted in the classroom from knowledge-based information to behavior-feeling oriented curriculums.[11]

What's more frightening is the testing that has changed to accommodate this shift from knowledge to affective learning. Affective learning is thoughts, feelings, behaviors, values, actions. Students are actually being "tracked" by computer on how they respond on these new exams. If the student is not performing toward the proper "outcomes," they will be remediated to the proper behavior, values, or feelings! This is the core of Outcome Based Education.[12]

David: Tell us what recently happened in California. California is used as an educational model throughout the U.S.

Susan: In September of this year it was reported that California fourth graders scored last in the nation in standardized reading, and over half had fallen below the national norms in math. Why? Apparently the educational elite decided to remove "rote learning" (memorization) and include "higher order thinking skills" into their classrooms. Two state task forces investigated the disastrous results and found that basic skills are missing: phonics had been ignored in reading and spelling omitted, too.[13] This is a good example of "actions (test scores) speak louder than words" (edu-babble of the educational elite)!

David: What is the agenda of Goals 2000? There is so much talk of it in the media.

Susan: Goals 2000 was a massive education bill that revamped our entire educational system. Congressman Dick Armey of Texas opposed this bill and explained it as such. It would:

1. Create a National School Board (appointed by the Clinton Administration).
2. Create a union-dominated skills board to develop "voluntary" national skill standards to be used by employers in hiring.
3. Create an opportunity to learn standards with mandatory standards on spending, curriculum, teacher salaries, etc.

4. Promote Outcome Based Education.
5. Promote multiculturalism.

David: What is that?

Susan: Multiculturalism is best explained by Congressman Armey:

> Americanism relates to our political foundation based on our Constitution, to our economic foundation based on free enterprise system, and our social order premised upon access to equal opportunity for all. The opposite view promotes multiculturalism—an excessive celebration of differences, with a cynical view of our nation's rich history.[14]

Goals 2000 also establishes non-academic goals for our schools. It violates federal law which prohibits the federal government from setting curricula!

Currently the Republicans in Congress are involved in axing the funding to Goals 2000 so that no money can be disbursed to make it a reality. Four states have turned down Goals 2000 money because they do not want the federal government dictating to them how they can run their schools! But there is other federal legislation that is as equally strangling as Goals 2000. H.R. 1816, the "Careers Bill," which was sponsored by two Republicans, would create a "work force development plan." The government would become responsible for your child's job placement. They will track students via computer and instead of them attending the "traditional" school, children will become part of a "one-stop career center" where they will be trained for designated job slots.[15]

David: What piece of advice can you give parents?

Susan: Listen. Read. Get involved. There are many fine organizations that you can send to for information, and they will assist you in networking with other concerned parents in your area. There are also excellent resources for reading about the education reform movement. There's more than meets the eye when it comes to your child's education. You get only one chance with them. Don't waste it!

In conclusion, if humanistic teachers are not deliberately promoting illiteracy, why would they want to introduce a curriculum without goals for children to achieve? New Age teachers are now saying that we should do away with the grading system of A, B, C, D, and F. They say that young people who do not make good grades may be emotionally affected, so in order to protect their emotions, we should not give grades. Any teacher with even half a brain knows that the way to get children motivated to learn is to reward them. If you take away the award system you will remove the child's desire to succeed.

Can you imagine trying to get people to give themselves to hard work and invest many years in training so they can compete in the Olympics, knowing there would be no gold, silver, or bronze medal to win? Would these athletes compete if they were not rewarded? Every time you have a sporting event there are winners and losers. How exciting would these events be if the contestants neither won nor lost? People would soon become bored and quit attending them.

In the very same way, if you remove the opportunity for children to succeed or fail they, too, will become bored and, in no time at all, will lose their desire to learn. *I* know that and I'm sure most *educators* know that as well. Besides, we can learn valuable lessons from our failures. So why are these New Age teachers trying to produce illiteracy? The answer is really quite simple: *illiterate people are easier to control.* If the only thing you know is what the liberal media tells you, wouldn't you think just like them? And so, while Christians are being called "ignorant" people, it is, in fact, our "literacy" that's upsetting those who want to silence us.

ORIGIN DIJTORTION—
IN JEARCH
OF THE MIJJING LINK

If you want to confuse someone about the future, you must first confuse them about the past. Tell a child he's a child of the King and he'll act like a child of the King. Tell him he came from a monkey and treat him like an animal, and you have today's public school system.

Shattered marriages. Sexual promiscuity. Abortion. Euthanasia. Rampant homosexuality. Racism. Youth in rebellion. What is happening to our world? And why? I may astonish you, but belief in the evolution of life is the source of much of our present society's confusion and waning morality. Evolutionism in all its forms has become so firmly entrenched that it now tears at the very fabric of our moral structure.[1]

And God said, Let us make man in our image, after our likeness: and let them have dominion over the fish of the sea, and over the fowl of the air, and over the cattle, and over all the earth, and over every creeping thing that creepeth upon the earth (Gen. 1:26).

This is where evolutionists and creationists are diametrically opposed. Evolution teaches that man came from animals and that out of a need, man created God. The creationist believes that man was created by God; he didn't come from animals. Man was created in the image of God, so today we have millions of people in an identity crisis because they have lost the true identity of God, their Creator, through evolutionary teaching. There is only one purpose for evolution, and that is to disprove the existence of God.

Myriads of people are being shipwrecked in spiritually defiled waters and don't understand why they are drowning. They cling to lifeboat "Science" in the hope that its answers to the origin of life, backed up by impressive credentials and high-sounding assurances, will rescue them and provide them with the stability and meaning that they are desperately searching for. They have been hooked by false claims that the world began without supernatural intervention, and assume that this all-too-familiar theory is verifiable fact supported by scientific data.[2]

You might say that the science book has replaced the Bible in infallibility:

The *Humanist Magazine* carried an articled entitled "Three Cheers for Our Secular State," by Paul Blanchard. He states, "Our schools may not teach Johnny to read properly, but the fact that Johnny is in school until he is sixteen tends to lead toward the elimination of religious superstition. The average American child now acquires a high school education, and this militates against Adam and Eve and all other alleged myths of alleged history."[3]

You must understand that in schools today, it's more important to be politically correct than it is to be properly educated. Hitler turned the educational system of his day into a system of indoctrination, and we're seeing it happen again. I have some very dear friends, Kenny and Karen, who live in Tallahassee, Florida. Last year while their daughter Michelle was attending a public school, she learned very quickly the importance of being politically correct in the classroom. Karen told me this story:

"In the spring of 1995 at the middle school my daughter attended, the eighth grade participated in a 'peace' unit. During a six-week period, all the classes used this theme. In language arts, much of their focus was on the dress and music of the 1960s. (What was so 'peaceful' about the 1960s???!!!) The specific assignment that disturbed me the most was in algebra. The worksheet began with a statement/figure of how much money was spent on armaments in a certain amount of time during the Vietnam War. The questions that followed had the students calculate how much this was per hour, per second, per day, written in decimal form, rounded to the nearest million, etc. The figure is astronomical!! The final question asked the student how he/she would decide to spend that amount of money in the budget if it was their decision. Examples were given such as ozone layer research, rain forest preservation, feeding the homeless . . . (environmental hogwash and over-population hoopla).

"My daughter's answer divided the money among preventive medical research, saving the babies, and military forces to protect our national sovereignty. This was totally 'politically INcorrect'!! Of course, she never brought the graded paper home, but she thinks she made a D on the assignment and the 'academic' portion of the paper was correct. This was in spite of a phone call to her teacher explaining that she couldn't be graded on her 'opinion' part of the paper." Karen regretted that she never pursued that issue further.

Classroom time today is increasingly being used for indoctrination, and students are being intimidated by teachers who grade them on their "political correctness" instead of their academic skills. Why is this happening? John Dunphy, in *Humanist Magazine*, sounds the battle cry for teachers to man their battle stations for war.

> The battle for human kind's future must be waged and won in the public school classroom by teachers who correctly perceive their role as the proselytizers of a new faith. . . . These teachers must embody the same selfless dedication as the most rabid fundamentalist preachers, for they will be ministers of another sort, utilizing a classroom instead of a pulpit to convey humanist values in whatever subject they teach regardless of the educational level.[4]

Then the humanists or TV reinforce evolution through Barney, Power Rangers, etc. At this point, some of you are wondering, "What is a humanist?" A humanist is a socially accepted and politically correct name for an atheist. Their main goal is to eliminate the existence of God from our society. Their most important weapon in this fight is evolution. Humanists will teach evolution as fact, not theory. A "theory" has more than one possible answer. A "fact" leaves no room for other conclusions. If evolution were taught as a theory, then other theories would have to be presented. Yet, the students are never given an optional view.

Humanism states that evolution is a scientific deduction based on scientific data, and that creationism is based on a myth derived from a religious belief. I do not claim to be a scholar in the field of creationism versus evolution, but I can say that evolution is not scientific. Let me give you an example. According to evolution, the earth is billions of years old. There is one problem with this theory that is taught as fact. Science tells us that the sun is 96 million miles away from the earth. The distance between the earth and the sun is critical, for if the earth were only ten percent further from the sun, it would freeze, and if the earth were only ten percent closer to the sun, it would be too hot for life to exist here. Scientists and astronomers will tell you that the sun is burning away toward its core. Given this fact of science, how big must the sun have been a billion years ago as it burned toward its core? Even if it burned away just one mile a year, a sun that big would have burned up the earth!

God is a wonderful Creator. You see, the "missing link" man should be looking for is not spelled a-p-e; it's spelled G-o-d.

REASONS YOUNG PEOPLE FIND THEMSELVES IN AN "IDENTITY CRISIS"

And God said, Let us make man in our image, after our likeness: and let them have dominion over the fish of the sea, and over the fowl of the air, and over the cattle, and over all the earth, and over every creeping thing that creepeth upon the earth. So God created man in his own image, in the image of God created he him; male and female created he them (Gen. 1:26–27).

Key statement: "The more I know about God, the more I will understand myself. I was made in God's image in the beginning. I've changed—not Him."

A. They try to find that person their parents told them they were.

(What Parents Say)	(What Teen Is Thinking)
1. You're a smart person	1. Why can't I answer life's questions?
2. You're a pretty girl.	2. My nose is too long, etc.
3. You're a good boy.	3. If they only knew.

B. They try to find that person their peers tell them they are. "He that walketh with wise men shall be wise: but a companion of fools shall be destroyed" (Prov. 13:20).

(What Their Peers Say)   *(What Teen Thinks)*

(What Their Peers Say)	*(What Teen Thinks)*
1. She is the life of the party.	1. I hate being plastic.
2. He sure is a crazy guy.	2. I have to be odd to be accepted.
3. He'll fight anybody.	3. I really don't want to fight but my friends expect it.

C. They have body changes. In two to three years a young person can change so much that they cannot adjust.

1. He grows twelve inches in two years. He becomes lanky and uncoordinated.
2. He goes from first tenor to low bass.
3. She has changed from a little girl to a young lady in two or three years. She goes from playing with dolls to dating.
4. They have problems with their complexion.
   a. No chocolate
   b. No sweets
   c. Wash face three times a day
   d. Clearasil in every home

D. They find a conflict between parent associations and peer associations. Until the teen years, most of their friends are okayed by the parents.

1. I'm going to find my own friends. "Make no friendship with an angry man; and with a furious man thou shalt not go: Lest thou learn his ways, and get a snare to thy soul" (Prov. 22:24–25).
2. Mom and Dad don't understand me.
3. My friends understand me.

Key statement: Teens pick friends according to the way they feel about themselves; low self-esteem may cause bad friendships.

E. They have to make major decisions for the first time.
1. Should I take biology?
2. Should I date a lost person?
3. Should I drink, do drugs, smoke, etc.?

Key statement: Many times the first decisions are bad ones; this may cause discouragement.

F. The future can be a discouragement to them.
1. What about a vocation?
2. What about college?
3. What about marriage and a family?

Key statement: If a teen does not know who he is, it is hard for him to know where he is going.

G. They want liberation without an alternate plan.
1. "Mom! Don't tell me what to do!"
2. "I can't wait until I'm my own boss!"

Key statement: This liberation usually turns into bondage; they become free to become addicted to drugs, alcohol, pornography, and other vices. The children of Israel prayed for hundreds of years for freedom only to want to go back to Egypt after being freed.

H. Their minds tell them they are adults, but their actions tell others they are still immature. This confuses them.

Key statement: When young people grow up too fast, they

surrender something they can never regain—childhood. This may be the reason they do not act their age as they grow older. They realize they can never return to their youth.

I. They meet pride and ego head on.
1. They become defensive.
2. They become defiant.
3. Their main goal is to please themselves.

Key statement: People usually do not think very highly of someone who thinks only of himself.

JUICIDE—CHILDREN FACING THE GRIM REAPER

Did you know that thirty young people attempt to commit suicide every thirty minutes? I was sitting in a pastor's study before I was to speak. Somehow, we got on the subject of suicide. He told me that he recently performed the funeral of a girl in his church. She was only a teenager trying to find answers. He said that during the funeral, the girl's mother told him something which she had felt to be strange.

After finding the body of her daughter, she called the police. When the investigator came to the home, he told the mother that even though he had never been in the girl's bedroom, he knew that when he did go in he would find one to three specific albums in her daughters record collection. And sure enough, when he went into the room he found those three albums in her collection.

Rock music, drugs, or alcohol are usually found at the scene of teen suicides. There have been lawsuits against rock musicians like Ozzy Osborne and Judas Priest. And yet, these cases have been thrown out of court every time. Rock musicians repeat the messages over and over with songs like:

1. *99 Ways To Die,* performed by Megadeth
2. *Suicide Solution,* performed by Ozzy Osborne
3. *Die Young, Stay Pretty,* performed by Debra Harry
4. *Looking Down the Barrel of a Gun,* performed by Anthrax
5. *I Hate Myself and Want To Die,* performed by Nirvana (These were not idle words for the lead singer Curt Cobain. He ended his own life by the act of suicide, shooting himself in the head.)

According to testimony given at a Parent Music Resource Center hearing before the Senate Commerce Committee on September 19, 1985, teenage suicides have gone up a whopping 300 percent in the last thirty years, while the adult rate has stayed the same.[1]

Is this by accident or is it by design? This is a question we may never be able to answer. I do find it interesting that with so many young people attempting to commit suicide, and so many rockers promoting it, no one has been able to win a case in court. These rockers hide behind the First Amendment of free speech.

Several years back I was asked to debate a lawyer from People for the American Way on the First Amendment rights of these rock stars. The attorney started the program off by saying, "We live in America. We can say whatever we want. We have the First Amendment rights!" To that I responded, "The First Amendment rights were never given to protect an illegal act." These are a few examples I gave him:

- I cannot walk into a crowded public building and yell, "Fire!" I would be arrested.
- I cannot call a daycare center and tell the director that I planted a bomb in the building and they

had better get the children out. If children were killed in the stampede, could I be protected by the First Amendment? No.

- I cannot call the White House and tell the switchboard operator that I am going to kill the president. Why? Because the First Amendment does not allow me to say things that can produce harm to people or property.
- I asked the lawyer, "Do you believe that Charles Manson should be released from prison?" This, of course, was a loaded question because Charles Manson has never been convicted of killing one person. He has been in prison for over twenty-five years because he inspired people to kill.

It has been estimated that a quarter of a million teens try to kill themselves every year. Something that should alarm us even more is the fact that children, even before their teen years, are now committing suicide!

"An 8-year-old makes a will. It reads: I want to not live no more. Mickey gets my bank and mommey my stampbook."[2] Another report reads like this: "4-year-old David wrapped himself in a blanket and set it on fire. When asked why, he answered, 'Because David is a bad boy, there will be no more David.'"[3]

If you want more proof that rock musicians influence young people, consider these cases:

Heavy Metal Related Crime

1. **Influence:** Metallica **Date:** January 1988
   Occurrence: Murder/Suicide **Place:** Newark, NJ
   Subject: Tom Sullivan, 14 **Interests:** Satanism
   Weapon: Boy Scout knife **Victim:** Mother
   Source: *Detroit News,* **Etc:** Sullivan com-
       1/13/88   mitted suicide

2. **Influence:** Judas Priest, Black Sabbath
   Occurrence: Ritual killing
   Subject: Richard Kasso, 17
   Weapon: Knife, stabbed 17 times
   Source: *Star Telegram,* 7/15/84

   Date: July 1984
   Place: Long Island, NY
   Interests: Satanism/drugs
   Victim: Gary Lauwers, 17
   Etc: Kasso committed suicide in jail

3. **Influence:** Ozzy Osborne
   Occurrence: Ritual murder
   Subjects: Terry Belcher, Bob McIntyre
   Weapon: Leather boot lace/ strangled
   Source: *Weekly World News,* 7/26/88

   Date: July 1988
   Location: Douglas Co., GA
   Interests: (?)
   Victim: Theresa Simmons, 17
   Etc: Animal sacrifices, blood tasting

4. **Influence:** Judas Priest
   Occurrence: Suicide
   Subject: Ray Belknap
   Weapon: (?)
   Source: *Las Vegas Gazette,* 10/9 & 11/88 Menconi Ministries

   Date: 12/23/85
   Location: Nevada
   Interests: Heavy Metal
   Victim: Ray Belknap
   Etc: Stain Class Album

5. **Influence:** Judas Priest
   Occurrence: Attempted Suicide
   Subject: James Vance
   Weapon: (?)
   Source: *Reno Gazette,* 10/9 & 11/88 Menconi Ministries

   Date: 12/23/85
   Location: Nevada
   Interests: Heavy Metal
   Victim: James Vance
   Etc: Stain Class Album

6. **Influence:** Ozzy Osborne **Date:** 1984
   Occurrence: Suicide **Location:** Los Angeles
   Subject: John McCollum **Interests:** Heavy Metal
   Weapon: .22 pistol **Victim:** John McCollum
   Source: *London Free Press,* **Etc:** Family attempts to sue
   1/14/86 Ozzy Osborne

7. **Influence:** WASP, Metal **Date:** (?)
   Church, White
   Snake, AC/DC,
   Black Sabbath,
   DIO
   Occurrence: Suicide **Location:** New Haven, VT
   Subject: Michelle Kimball **Interests:** Satan worship
   Weapon: Shot in the head **Victim:** Michelle Kimball
   Source: *Las Vegas Review* **Etc:** Michell made pact with
   Journal, 3/26/88 her boyfriend, who lived.

8. **Influence:** AC/DC **Date:** (?)
   Occurrence: Suicide **Location:** Kerr Co., TN
   Subject: Dennis Bartts **Interest:** Heavy Metal
   Weapon: Hanging tool **Victim:** Dennis Bartts
   Source: *N.F.D. Journal,* **Etc:**
   11/85

9. **Influence:** The Wall **Date:** February 1986
   (Pink Floyd)
   Occurrence: Ritualistic **Location:** Delafield, WI
   suicide
   Subject: Philip Morton **Interests:** Occult
   Weapon: Bed sheet over a **Victim:** Philip Morton
   door
   Source: Waukesha Co. **Etc:** Found hanging in
   Chief ME, front of a skull and
   Paul Hibbard a lit candle.[4]

ſUICIDE—
NOT A NEW PROBLEM

Most people do not realize that those living during biblical times had problems. Suicide has always been a way of escape for some. You see there are many who would tell you that the causes of suicide are broken homes, peer pressure, or fear of the future. (I am told that some commit suicide because they are afraid that they may die of a nuclear bomb.) Probably the most common response people give as to the cause of suicide is that the victims were going to do it anyway.

Some would ask, "Can the Bible shed some light on this current issue?" The answer is, yes. There are seven people in the Bible who killed themselves.

1. Abimelech (son of Jerubbaal): "Then he called hastily unto the young man his armourbearer, and said unto him, Draw thy sword, and slay me, that men say not of me, A woman slew him. And his young man thrust him through, and he died" (Judg. 9:54) Motive for death: **Pride.**

2. Samson: "And Samson said, Let me die with the Philistines. And he bowed himself with all his might; and the house fell upon the lords, and upon all the people that were therein" (Judg. 16:30). Motive for death: **Revenge.**

3. Saul: "Then said Saul unto his armourbearer, Draw thy sword, and thrust me through . . . But his armourbearer would not. . . . Therefore Saul took a sword, and fell upon it" (1 Sam. 31:4). Motive for death: **Fear.**

4. Saul's armourbearer: "And when his armourbearer saw that Saul was dead, he fell likewise upon his sword, and died with him" (1 Sam. 31:5). Motive for death: **Loyalty to his leader.**

5. Ahithophel: "And when Ahithophel saw that his counsel was not followed, he saddled his ass, and arose, and gat him home to his house, to his city, and put his household in order, and hanged himself, and died, and was buried in the sepulchre of his father" (2 Sam. 17:23). Motives for death: **Spiritual**—his plot against God's anointed had failed. **Psychological**—he felt he had to die because of his mistake (giving bad counsel).

6. Zimri: "And it came to pass, when Zimri saw that the city was taken, that he went into the palace of the king's house, and burnt the king's house over him with fire, and died" (1 Kings 16:18). Motive for death: **Hopelessness regarding the future.**

7. Judas: "And he cast down the pieces of silver in the temple, and departed, and went and hanged himself" (Matt. 27:5). Motive for death: **Guilt.**

The motives for suicide are still the same today.

○ **Pride.** These young people agree together to make a

pact of death and then their pride will not allow them to back out.

○ **Revenge.** Suicide victims often use revenge as a motive. Common statements are:

- "I'll show my parents!"
- "I'll show my girlfriend not to break anyone else's heart!"
- "I'll make them live with the guilt of my death for not doing things my way!"

○ **Fear of the consequences of failure.** Some may say, "Just look at my life—everything I've ever done has gone sour," or, "I guess I'd be better off just ending it." A businessman who made a bad decision resulting in a loss may commit suicide.

○ **Loyalty to a leader.** Need any more be said concerning cult groups like Jim Jones? How many young people have gone into a severe depression or have tried to commit suicide because rock idols have died? I am convinced that if a rock star were to commit suicide on stage and ask others to do so, not all of those present would walk out alive. But even if it did happen, some would still not believe that rock and roll can influence young people toward suicide.

○ **The feeling that they must die because of their mistakes.** I once heard a story of a man who committed immorality with a prostitute. He did not have the money to pay her so she claimed that he had raped her. The police showed up at his house to arrest him. His wife called him at work and told him the police were coming for him. The man called his pastor and asked him to stay with his family. He then took his gun, drove to the railroad tracks, and committed suicide. He felt that he could not live with his mistake.

O **Hopelessness regarding the future.** Elderly people will sometimes commit suicide because they feel that the future holds nothing for them.

O **Guilt.** Many people die because they blame themselves so much that they see no other way to find relief.

There is yet one more reason for suicides among people today, but you will not find this reason taught in medical schools around this country. I believe that some (not all) who commit suicide do so because of *demon possession.* It is interesting to note that as you observe the rise of satanic worship and occult teachings, you will also note the rise of suicide. There have been direct links to suicide among people who play Dungeons & Dragons. I believe this theory can be backed by Scripture (Matt. 17:14–21; Mark 9:14–29; Luke 9:37–43a). The boy in these passages was simply called Lunatic, yet he was not crazy. The boy was driven to commit suicide by burning and by drowning, yet he was not suicidal. He was possessed. Maybe you will take time to study these passages during your own devotions.

Finally, the Bible tells us that during the time of the Tribulation, there will be people who will try to commit suicide but won't be able to do so (Rev. 9:6).

As long as people seek after this world, they will constantly come up empty. And as long as people seek righteousness, they will always come away full.

IDENTIFYING THE CAJUALTIEJ OF THIJ JEXUAL REVOLUTION

Several years ago, I had an opportunity to visit a training facility for Arabian horses. The trainer was a member of the church where I had spoken and had offered me a free ride, so I took it. The horses in that stable were beautiful and well-trained. The horse I rode was as smooth as silk. It had a better ride than my fifth-wheel trailer. After the ride, we proceeded to wipe down the horses and put them away.

I looked in one stall and saw a magnificent horse. It was a black stallion. His coat was shiny and his muscles well defined. I turned to the trainer and said, "That is a beautiful horse," to which the trainer responded, "He isn't worth the gun powder it would take to blow him up." Confused by her statement, I asked her to explain what she meant. She said, "Just go and stand by the stall."

Well, I did, but not for long. The horse started to rear up and hoof the gate. I was surprised to see such unprovoked anger. I asked, "What in the world is wrong with him?" I'll never forget what she told me. She said, "David, the reason that horse is uncontrollable is because his owners bred him too early, and now all he thinks about is sex and violence."

This seemed easy for me to understand. I have worked with young people for over eighteen years, and I see the same thing with young people if they engage in sex too early in their life. They have a hard time thinking about anything but sex, and often they become violent.

Today, sex educators insist on teaching sex to children before the body and mind are ready to understand it. Even in pre-school, dolls have to be anatomically correct.

Casualty #1—Those Exposed to Sex Education

George Grant, in his book *The Family Under Siege,* tells of an experience a 15-year-old girl named Catherine had during a health, sex-education class. Her health teacher brought in a representative from the local "woman's clinic" to talk about sex, contraception, pregnancy, and abortion.

"I've never seen pornography before," Catherine admitted. "But this film was worse than what I could have ever imagined hard-core pornography to be."

The film was extremely explicit. An unashamedly brash couple fondled each other in preparation for intercourse. The camera continually zoomed in for close-up shots on sweaty bodies, caressing, kissing, stroking, petting, embracing. At the height of passion, the camera fixed on the woman's hands as she tore open a condom package and began to slowly unroll its contents onto her partner.

"I wanted to look away or cover my eyes, but I couldn't," Catherine said. "I just stared at the screen—in horror."

When the lights came back on, the entire class was visibly shaken. With wide eyes, the youngsters sat speechless and amazed. But their guest was entirely unperturbed.

"She began to tell us that everything that we'd just seen was totally normal and totally good," Catherine remembered. "She said that the couple obviously had a caring, loving, and responsible relationship because they took proper precautions against conception and disease."

At that, the speaker passed several packages of condoms around the room, one for each of the girls. She instructed the boys to hold up a finger so that the girls could practice contraceptive application. Already shell-shocked, the students did as they were told. But afterward, several of the girls began quietly sobbing, another girl ran out of the room and threw up, still another fainted. Mercifully, the class ended just a moment later.

"I have never been more humiliated in all my life," Catherine said. "I felt dirty and defiled after seeing the film. But then, when I had to put that thing on Billy's finger—well, it was horrible. It was like I'd been raped. Raped in my mind. Raped by my school."[1]

The way these classes are taught destroys the innocence of these children. It desensitizes young people. Once sex is role-played in the classroom there are no barriers to overcome when they are alone.

This is all done under the guise of safe sex. It is amazing that our government spends billions of dollars on safe sex while opposing those who try to teach abstinence. They are just assuming that teenagers will have sex. Because of their attitude toward sex, they are assuming correctly. This is why these statistics are not unbelievable:

Every thirty minutes . . .

- 60 teenage girls will become pregnant.
- 24 teenage girls will have an abortion.
- 15 teenage girls will give birth to illegitimate babies.

The number of girls becoming sexually active, when broken down by grades, looks something like this:

- 72 percent of twelfth graders are sexually active.
- 57 percent of eleventh graders are sexually active.
- 48 percent of tenth graders are sexually active.
- 40 percent of ninth graders are sexually active.

This last year, my daughter turned thirteen. On her birthday, I took her out on a "date" for a nice dinner. After the meal, I gave her a beautiful "promise" ring that her mother and I had bought for her. Before giving her the ring, I asked her to promise us that she would remain sexually pure until her wedding night. If she broke that promise, she would have to return the ring to us. That was a tear-filled evening for both of us. I told her that if she was ever tempted with impure thoughts or unwanted advances, just to look at the ring and think of her promise to us.

The sad thing is that many parents are putting their daughters on contraceptives at thirteen years of age. The difference between the sex educators and myself is that they want to believe that children are going to become sexually active. I want to believe that mine will not. Some may call my wife and me naive, but every day Christian couples get married and they experience sex for the first time in their lives.

Everyone has heard the saying, "Everybody is doing it!" for so long, we're starting to believe it ourselves. I like how one girl responded when her boyfriend said to her in a parked car, "Let's have sex. Everybody else is doing it!" The girl replied, "Well, if everybody else is doing it, you shouldn't have a hard time finding someone else to do it with!"

Giving a child contraceptives and expecting them not to use them is like giving your child a car and his own set of car keys, and then expecting him not to drive it.

Casualty #2—Those Who Are Exploited by Sex-Sellers

Lloyd Martin, officer in charge of the Sexually Exploited Child Unit of the Los Angeles Police Department, testified before the Arizona House Hearings on Pornography, Child Pornography, and Child Prostitution. His estimates were that between 40,000 and 50,000 children are involved in pornography and prostitution. He said that child exploitation is a thriving, multimillion dollar business. It was estimated that in 1982, the child sex industry made over 5 billion dollars.[2]

Casualty #3—Those Who Thought It Would Not Happen to Them

When I was growing up, there were venereal diseases. These were treated by medical science. A person in the 1960s and '70s could make a mistake and live to tell about it. In the 1980s and '90s, it's a different story. People who contract AIDS are without medical hope. AIDS crosses ethnic, religious, and social boundaries to infect on contact.

A very good example is "Magic" Johnson. He is, without a doubt, one of the greatest basketball players ever and he contracted this disease. Almost like the death of JFK, I can remember where I was when I heard this news. I was in a hotel room in Florida on the night of November 7, 1991. "Magic" Johnson stood behind a press platform and announced he had tested HIV positive.

This is the virus that leads to AIDS. While safe sex advocates preach safe sex, they are not being honest with children. Children are being told that sex is safe if the man wears a safety device called a condom. This is a bold-faced lie!

First of all, the AIDS virus is smaller than the pores in these latex devices, allowing them to travel right through the device. Secondly, they are not reliable.

> How can you have safe sex when condoms fail in over 14 percent of heterosexual relations, and 18 percent of homosexual relationships? And the rate is certain to be even higher for the young, inept teens, because condoms can slip and break. Additionally, New York City alone experienced a recall in November of 1990 for 750,000 defective condoms.[3]

Thirdly, the odds are growing every day.

> Dr. William A. Haseltine, a leading AIDS researcher at the Harvard School in Boston, has warned that the AIDS epidemic will produce an "enormous" and "frightening" effect on world health that public health officials may be relatively powerless to contain. Dr. Haseltine . . . painted one of the most frightening pictures of AIDS yet put forth by any prominent scientist. He noted that

perhaps a million people in the United States, and conceivably 20 million worldwide, had already been infected with the virus, even though only a small percentage had yet become sick.[4]

Young people today are dying, thinking it will never happen to them. There are those who believe that AIDS was a created virus to control the world population. I don't know if it was a plan or an accident, but AIDS is playing—and will continue to play—a major role in decreasing world population.

Isn't it interesting that on one hand, the media downplays the fact that AIDS victims should have been isolated. They claim the only way to contract AIDS is through sex. Yet, on the other hand, they say if we do not find a cure it could devastate the world's population. This is the question: Is AIDS hard to get? The answer to that question is a sad one. No, it isn't hard to get. AIDS is easily contracted by anyone.

Recommended Reading from the Book Shelf

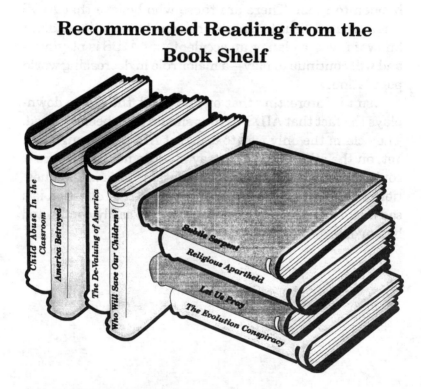

America Betrayed, Marlin Maddoux
Child Abuse In the Classroom, Phyllis Schlaffly
The De-Valuing of America, William J. Bennett
Who Will Save Our Children?, Beverly LaHaye
Subtle Serpent, Darylann Whitemarsh and Bill Reism
Religious Apartheid, John Whitehead
Let Us Pray, William J. Murray
The Evolution Conspiracy, Caryl Matrisciana and Roger Oakland

Section III

ENLIGHTENMENT FROM THE NEW AGE

THE CROSS-DRESSING OF GOD

If you're not careful the New Agers will perform a sex change on God right before your eyes! Recently I was speaking at a rally in Milwaukee. Everything was going as planned until I made a statement that referred to God in the male gender. A man quickly jumped to his feet and started to rebuke me. He said that God is male *and* female and quoted Genesis 1:27 which says, "So God created man in his own image, in the image of God created he him; male and female created he them." The man proceeded to tell the audience that God has a male side and a female side.

Let me explain this verse. Man and woman were created holy, after the holiness of God. The passage he quoted has nothing to do with gender, but it has everything to do with holiness and dominion, characteristics that distinguish man from any other animal.

> And God said, Let us make man in our image, after our likeness: and let them have dominion over the fish of the sea, and over the fowl of the air, and over the cattle, and over all the earth, and over every creeping thing that creepeth upon the earth (Gen. 1:26).

You see, fish were created male and female, birds were created male and female, cattle were created male and female. If gender were the issue here, then God would have said that fish, birds, cattle, and creeping things were made in His image. But He didn't. God said that *man* was created in His image. Man was different from all other creatures because he was created with the ability to be holy, even as God is holy. You will never see a cow praying. You will never find a fish repenting from sin. Only man was created in the likeness of God's holiness. After the fall, man became sinful and needed to be regenerated. The animal kingdom can never be restored to holiness because they were never created holy, as was man.

You may be wondering where this fellow at the meeting got such an idea. Well, he was an environmentalist. Earlier that day he told us that he had attended a green peace rally. Environmentalism is often used by the New Age movement as a "store-front" to introduce people to the female deity. She is called the goddess Gaia, or Mother Earth. Christians need to be aware that witches and occultists believe in a female deity and pass it off as a Christian doctrine. There is a major movement in Christianity to accept both the male and female deity. There's even a new Bible translation that refers to God as Father/Mother. Mainline denominations are now accepting Sophia as a substitute for Jesus.

The male/female God force does not come from Christian teaching. It comes from Taoism, a Chinese philosophy. The symbol for Taoism is the yin yang (see yin yang in the chapter on New Age symbols). The yin yang principle says that the male and female are always at war with one another. God is not at war within Himself. The male side is not at war with the female side. The God of Christianity is not a dichotomy. He is a Trinity in perfect holiness. Even when Jesus was on earth, He was here to do the will of the Father in Heaven.

The goddess issue is not avoided in the Word of God. In fact, we clearly see from Scripture that the purpose of the goddess belief was not to bring people to Jehovah, but to turn their hearts away from Him.

> But since we left off to burn incense to the queen of heaven, and to pour out drink offerings unto her, we have wanted all things, and have been consumed by the sword and by the famine. And when we burned incense to the queen of heaven, and poured out drink offerings unto her, did we make her cakes to worship her, and pour out drink offerings unto her, without our men? (Jer. 44:18–19).

It's interesting to note that they worshipped without their men! You see, these women were feminists. Strangely enough, it's the feminists who are pushing for the acceptance of goddess worship today! Any book about witchcraft will show you that they all worship a female deity.

Let me give you one good example of this from a book entitled, *Changing of the Gods*.

> I have one close friend for whom the father-god is still very important, even though she is now a worshiper of the goddess in the Sisterhood of Wicca [wicca is another name for witch]. My friend readily admits that she still needs the father. "I need the goddess to love and pray to. But I need the male god to scream at for making life so sad. I know this is a primitive way to think, to make the goddess all good and the male god all bad. But this is how I feel."[1]

As you can clearly see, the ultimate end of believing that God is male and female is to turn hearts away from the male deity. Christianity and goddess worship cannot live in harmony. In Acts 19, the Apostle Paul had a run-in with the followers of the goddess Diana while in Ephesus.

Taking the theory that God is both male and female to its fullest extent, one would have to conclude that, if we were created in God's image (male and female as New Agers teach), there must be a male/female side within each one of us. So if every individual is male/female then homosexuality makes perfect sense. Satan would be a great chess player because he has a tremendous way of disguising his moves. And believe me, his moves are always well thought out. Every church that's been deceived by the Devil into believing that God has both male and female gender, has also opened its arms to the homosexual movement.

DAYS OF OUR PAST LIVES, OR IS REINCARNATION BIBLICALLY SOUND?

The Devil has a very crafty way of redefining words. He has had a field day with "born again" in the New Age movement. This is a biblical phrase.

> Jesus answered, Verily, verily, I say unto thee, Except a man be born of water and of the Spirit, he cannot enter into the kingdom of God. That which is born of the flesh is flesh; and that which is born of the Spirit is spirit. Marvel not that I said unto thee, Ye must be born again (John 3:5–7).

There are two different births:

1. The physical birth. The water sack that surrounds the baby in the mother's womb must burst before the child is born.

2. The spiritual birth. This is called regeneration. "Born again" has been redefined by the New Agers to mean born over and over again through the process of reincarnation. Shirley MacLaine claims that she has been born again 110 times, meaning that she has had 110 previous lives.

John 3:5–7 is not the only scripture that Satan takes out of context and perverts to promote reincarnation. The following texts are used by New Agers to "prove" reincarnation:

1. The man born blind. "And as Jesus passed by, he saw a man which was blind from his birth. And his disciples asked him, saying, Master, who did sin, this man, or his parents, that he was born blind?" (John 9:1–2).

First of all, the question that New Agers would ask at this point is, "This man was born blind. How could his sin have caused his blindness unless he lived in a previous life?" They say that this proves the disciples believed in reincarnation or they would not have posed the question.

Let's take a minute to address this point. First of all, the disciples were asking a question. This does not mean that they believed it. There are many people who ask me questions about witchcraft. This does not mean they are witches. They are just looking for answers.

Secondly, New Agers will never point out that this was a twofold question: Who did sin, 1) the man? or 2) his parents? Reincarnation does not teach that sin is transferred to you by others but that you, alone, determine your karma. Your parents cannot affect it, so New Agers only emphasize the first part of verse two. They never address the second part which says, ". . . or his parents?" Judaism teaches that the sins of the parents are transferred to the children. So, in essence, the disciples said, "Jesus, why was this man born blind? Is the answer found in reincarnation, that teaches he sinned in a past life; or in Judaism, which teaches that the sins of the parents were responsible?" If

Jesus had believed in reincarnation, He would have used this opportunity to explain karmic law. But He didn't.

Instead, Jesus answered in verse 3, "Neither hath this man sinned, nor his parents: but that the works of God should be made manifest in him." His explanation had nothing to do with personal sin, nor the transferal of sin. It dealt with God showing His mercy to heal the sick.

2. The reincarnation of Elijah. Some time ago, a man asked me to answer a question that was bothering him. He said, "I was listening to a man on the radio today and he was talking about reincarnation. This Christian lady called in and tried to set this man straight. But he quoted Luke 1:17, 'And he [John the Baptist] shall go before him [Jesus] in the spirit and power of Elias [or Elijah], to turn the hearts of the fathers to the children, and the disobedient to the wisdom of the just; to make ready a people prepared for the Lord.'"

According to the New Age movement, this proves that John the Baptist was the reincarnation of Elijah, the prophet. Does this verse reinforce their position? Let's see.

○ John denied it himself. "And they asked him, What then? Art thou Elias? And he saith, I am not. Art thou that prophet? And he answered, No" (John 1:21).

○ The Jews were indifferent to John's death. If the Jews really had believed the doctrine of reincarnation, as the New Agers claim they did, and if they really had accepted John the Baptist as the Old Testament prophet reborn, Herod would never have gotten away with killing him. The Jews would have risen up in protest.

3. Was Jesus the reincarnation of Elijah? In Matthew

16:13–15 we read, "When Jesus came into the coasts of Caesarea Philippi, he asked his disciples, saying, Whom do men say that I the Son of man am? [Jesus knew who He was and is.] And they said, Some say that thou art John the Baptist: some, Elias; and others, Jeremias, or one of the prophets. He saith unto them, But whom say ye that I am?" (Jesus didn't care what others were saying. He wanted to know if the disciples had the right answer.)

Peter did not jump up and say, "Elijah!" That answer belonged to the Devil's children. He didn't say, "Jeremiah." That, too, would have been wrong. Peter had a habit of putting his foot in his mouth, but this time he knew the right answer. In verse 16 we read, "And Simon Peter answered and said, Thou art the Christ, the Son of the living God." Listen to the response of Jesus to this answer. "And Jesus answered and said unto him, Blessed art thou, Simon Barjona: for flesh and blood hath not revealed it unto thee, but my Father which is in heaven" (vs. 17).

Again, if the Jews really had believed in reincarnation they would never have had Jesus crucified because they would have killed an honored prophet.

4. Has Elijah ever reincarnated? No. This is totally contrary to the New Agers own belief about reincarnation. Reincarnation teaches that you recycle into another life "after death." The problem is: Elijah never died!

> And it came to pass, as they still went on, and talked, that, behold, there appeared a chariot of fire, and horses of fire, and parted them both asunder; and Elijah went up by a whirlwind into heaven (2 Kings 2:11).

Another illustration is found in Matthew 17 where Elijah and Moses appeared to Jesus, Peter, James, and John on the Mount of Transfiguration. Neither of these two men had ever reincarnated (gone on to live other lives as many different people). When they appeared on the mountain, they were the same individuals as they had been many generations before when they lived and walked on the earth in their own day.

> ... It is appointed unto men once to die, but after this the judgment (Heb. 9:27).

NEW AGE TERMS

These are teachings according to the New Age movement:

A Course in Miracles. A popular, three-volume set of instructions on New Age beliefs. These writings were given by automatic handwriting. The spirit author goes by the name of Jesus. "... There be some that trouble you, and would pervert the gospel of Christ. But though we, or an angel from heaven, preach any other gospel unto you than that which we have preached unto you, let him be accursed" (Gal. 1:7–8).

Alchemy. God-like attributes that can alter nature.

Altered states of consciousness. A state of mind that allows one to contact demonic spirits.

Animal guide. New Age teachers believe that spirits take the form of animals, but we believe this to be demonic manifestations.

Ascended masters. Demon spirits that claim they lived before on earth and are now willing to teach you and guide your life. (This is taught in *The Lion King*.)

Attitudinal healing. By changing your attitude, you can change your health.

Aquarian age. A time that New Agers claim we are living in, where the spiritual awakening of man has now come.

Aura. A force field of lights that surround the body.

Automatic handwriting. A writing of a text supposedly written totally by a spirit through the hands of a man or woman.

Avatar. In the Hindu faith, people are taught that there are perfect spiritual leaders who have attained deity. The Bible teaches us that all our righteousness is as filthy rags to God. "But we are all as an unclean thing, and all our righteousnesses are as filthy rags; and we all do fade as a leaf; and our iniquities, like the wind, have taken us away" (Isa. 64:6).

Biofeedback. The use of special electronic equipment, plus mental exercises such as visualization and meditation, to influence psychological responses. Biofeedback is not bad if it is performed correctly, but New Age practitioners use it as a spring board into altered states of consciousness.

Born again. To a New Ager, it means being reincarnated.

Buddhism. An Eastern religion that combines meditation, chanting, and rituals. They claim Christ as a "master," but not as the one true God. They have many gods.

Centering. Another word for "meditation" used by the New Age movement.

Chakras. Hindus teach that there are seven energy pockets, or chakras, that start at the base of the spine and end at the top of the head. They claim that each chakra has its own color and rate of vibration, and that the lotus position helps to align these energy pockets.

Channeling. This occurs when the person's body is used by a demon spirit to communicate a message. The New Age movement uses the word "channeling" instead of "possession." The first spirit channeler was Satan. He had no human being to work through so he used a serpent.

Co-creation. Man creates his own reality.

Crystal power. The New Age movement believes crystals can give off energy that will heal, control dreams, and transmit information, such as a crystal ball.

Divination. The art of foretelling the future. Some use dreams, tea leaves, Ouija boards, astrology, etc. Demons cannot foretell the future. They can only manipulate circumstances so that it looks like they knew what was going to happen. If psychics can foretell the future, why don't they win the Lotto every week? Scriptures to refute this are:

> If there arise among you a prophet, or a dreamer of dreams, and giveth thee a sign or a wonder, And the sign or the wonder come to pass, whereof he spake unto thee, saying, Let us go after other gods, which thou hast not known, and let us serve them; Thou shalt not hearken unto the words of that prophet, or that dreamer of dreams: for the LORD your God proveth you, to know whether ye love the LORD your God with all your heart and with all your soul (Deut. 13:1–3).

> There shall not be found among you any one that maketh his son or his daughter to pass through the fire, or that useth divination, or an observer of times, or an enchanter, or a witch, Or a charmer, or a consulter with familiar spirits, or a wizard, or a necromancer. For all that do these things are an abomination unto the LORD: and because of these abominations the LORD thy God doth drive them out from before thee (Deut. 18:10–12).

Dolphins. The New Age teachers believe that dolphins can be channeled in order to help man in his survival.

Dream catchers. An Indian-made device that is supposed to control you and your child's dreams. (It is becoming very fashionable to put this device in a bedroom.)

Elementals. Forces of nature that witches believe they can control. There are five: earth, wind, fire, water, and spirit. (Children learned about these through *Pocahontas* and *Captain Planet.*)

Earth temples. These are sacred sites that New Agers believe contain extra psychic power presence, such as Stonehenge. (The Power Rangers taught this belief to children in *Mighty Morphin Power Rangers, the Movie.*)

Education. New Age teaching that supersedes physical science by way of supernatural science.

Energy. Inner energy can be altered by self-will and New Age techniques such as crystals. The energy force inside of man may be referred to as the yin yang.

Gargoyles. These are grotesque stone figures most commonly found on gothic buildings. Superstition has it that gargoyles frighten away evil spirits. We as Christians do not believe that. We believe that only God can protect us.

God. The basic belief of the New Age movement is pantheism: God is all and all is God. Other gods can be added without much problem. The New Age movement can accept other beliefs of gods, also.

Goddess worship. New Agers, as well as Wiccans, believe in a female deity as opposed to the Christian belief in a male deity. There are many different goddesses that they worship, not just one. (Gaia is the most popular. She is taught in education as Mother Earth. Children are taught by her daily in the cartoon, *Captain Planet.*)

Guided imagery. It is the releasing of your imagination to a physical teacher or spirit to help you grow and develop in your understanding of New Age ideas.

Hinduism. Another Eastern religion that worships many gods and uses meditation for spiritual awakening.

Human potential movement. You can be successful if you think it into reality. Christians believe we can do all things through Christ which strengthen us (Phil. 4:13)

Hypnosis. An altered state of consciousness. By using hypnosis a practitioner is able, through suggestions, to help a patient recall things in their past. (There are some Christians who believe this to be okay. I, personally, would never yield my will and consciousness to another person. The Bible tells us we are to be controlled by the person of the Holy Spirit of God.)

Inner child. The New Age movement claims that the inner self needs to be awakened in order to grow spiritually. Christianity teaches that we are to crucify the flesh and have no confidence in it (see Galatians 5:24).

Karmic law. This is a cycle which the New Age movement claims alters your next life. Karmic law means: If you do good in this life, you will be elevated in your next life. If you are bad in this life, you will descend in your next life. Christians do not believe in reincarnation. The Bible teaches that it is appointed unto man once to die (see Hebrews 9:27). The problem with karmic law is, as with any law, you must have a law-giver. The New Age movement does not believe in a personal God who keeps records. Without a law-giving process, we could drive 100 miles an hour and not be wrong.

Levitation. It is the defiance of the law of gravity. In seances, tables may rise and trumpets might float around the room. Peoples' bodies have been reported to lift off the ground. Aladdin's magic carpet is an example of levitation.

Mandalas. Visual symbols used as aids to meditation.

Mantra. Holy names of Hindu deities used in transcendental meditation.

Martial arts. A skill developed for use in self defense. Martial arts for self-defense is not wrong, yet many believers in Eastern religions use it as a way of teaching their religious beliefs. (Like Ninja Turtles, who use martial arts to teach everything from crystal power to mental telepathy; or the Power Rangers, who teach contacting animal spirits for power.)

Master. This is a teacher who has mastered the occult system of belief and can teach others what he/she has learned.

Meditation. An altered state of consciousness that allows a person to go beyond the physical and mental state to achieve spiritual enlightenment. The difference between Christian meditation and Eastern meditation is that Eastern meditation has you empty yourself so that you can be controlled by your own mental will, or a spirit. Bible meditation has you fill yourself with God's Word, and calm yourself with God's promises.

Mystical experiences. These are experiences that the New Age movement uses to validate their belief system.

Necromancer. A person who tries to communicate with the dead. Scripture that refutes this is Deuteronomy 18:10–12 (see "divination").

New Age subliminal programming. The use of audio tapes which contain subliminal, or hidden, messages recorded outside the area of conscious awareness that can be learned while you listen to something else on the same tape. New Agers claim that these subliminal messages can help you to stop smoking, cure eating disorders, and become successful while listening to the sound of waves, etc.

Out-of-body experience. This is the belief that you can leave your body and travel to places and know things impossible for you to know. This is done by demonic suggestion. Demons know a lot of things you don't know and through mind control they can get you to hallucinate these things into reality.

Parapsychology. Incorporating scientific methodology and expecting supernatural results. Examples: telepathy, psychic healing, etc.

Planitarization. This is another word for global consciousness; bringing the world into spiritual oneness. According to the Bible, in the book of Revelation, this one-world system will be ushered in by the False Prophet.

Progressive relaxation. An altered state of mind which the New Agers claim will elevate learning of physical and spiritual truths.

Pyramid power. The Egyptians were avid students of the occult. They had many gods and demonic spirits that surrounded them. They taught that the dimensions of the pyramids were a perfect conductor for metaphysical powers of the universe.

Reincarnation. This is the circle of life. If you are good in this life, you ascend in your next life. If you are bad in this life, you descend in your next life (see "karmic law"). This is taught in movies like *Ghost, Casper,* and *The Lion King.* Scripture that refutes this is Hebrews 9:27, "And as it is appointed unto men once to die, but after this the judgment."

Salvation. New Agers do not believe in salvation. Salvation to a New Ager may mean salvaging your life potential by gaining knowledge of the occult. Salvation to a Christian means that you realize you are a sinner and need a Savior. Christ died for our sins. Without the shedding of blood, there is no remission of sin (see Hebrews 9:22).

Self-esteem education. It is an education program that makes you feel more in control. You are in charge. (There is nothing wrong with feeling good about yourself. You are God's creation. But the biblical way to success is that we must decrease, and Christ must increase—John 3:30.)

Self-realization. This means you realize that you, yourself, are a god. This is an age-old lie of the Devil. Satan told Eve in Genesis 3:5, "For God doth know that in the day ye eat thereof, then your eyes shall be opened, and ye shall be as gods, knowing good and evil."

Shaman. This is another term for "witch doctor."

Sin. To a New Ager, sin means falling short of your human potential. To a Christian, sin means that we have broken God's law and must be punished (see Romans 3:23; 6:23).

Spirit lovers. Succubus and incubus spirits. The succubus spirit is a demon who supposedly materializes as a woman to have sexual relationships with men. The incubus spirit is a demon that supposedly materializes as a man and enters into sexual relationships with women, sometimes occurring in dreams. According to legend, trolls represent these vile spirits. To learn more about succubus and incubus spirits and trolls, see my book, *Fourteen Things Witches Hope Parents Never Find Out.*[1]

And it came to pass, when men began to multiply on the face of the earth, and daughters were born unto them, That the sons of God saw the daughters of men that they were fair; and they took them wives of all which they chose. And the Lord said, My spirit shall not always strive with man, for that he also is flesh: yet his days shall be an hundred and twenty years. There were giants in the earth in those days; and also after that, when the sons of God came in unto the daughters of men, and they bare children to them, the same became mighty men which were of old, men of renown. And God saw that the wickedness of man was great in the earth, and that every imagination of the thoughts of his heart was only evil continually. And it repented the Lord that he had made man on the earth, and it grieved him at his heart. And the Lord said, I will destroy man whom I have created from the face of the earth; both man, and beast, and the creeping thing, and the fowls of the air; for it repenteth me that I have made them (Gen. 6:1–7).

Taoism. A religious system that teaches that the super-natural can be altered by altering forces. The symbol for Taoism is the yin yang. Christians do not believe in forces. We believe in a personal God.

Transpersonal education. A teaching technique that encourages people to learn beyond their five senses. They are taught that a higher source of power is needed for ultimate knowledge.

Trolls. See "spirit lovers."

Values clarification. The New Age movement teaches that values are subjective. You are your own conscience. There are no absolutes, so if it feels good, do it. The Bible teaches that there are absolute truths and laws. Bible values are not used as a basis for values clarification.

Visualization. Mental concentration and direct imagery that allows one to succeed. There is nothing wrong with thinking through your situation. However, the New Age movement teaches that visualization goes beyond think-ing your way to success. It brings it into reality by the power of the mind.

Wicca. Another term for "witch." They use nature ele-mentals to perform magic (see "elementals"). "For re-bellion is as the sin of witchcraft, and stubbornness is as iniquity and idolatry. Because thou [Saul] hast rejected the word of the LORD, he hath also rejected thee from being king" (1 Sam. 15:23). By the way, God rejected Saul for consulting a witch (see I Samuel 28:7–18).

Yoga. This is an occult system of breathing techniques that obtain altered states of consciousness. As you read the manuals you will see that yoga is purely occultic. Again, even though it is taught as "science" and "exercise," yoga is a store-front for occultism. According to reports, Hitler was an avid student of yoga.

NEW AGE SYMBOLS

Ankh

This is a symbol for the goddess Osiris. It symbolizes sex, fertility, and reincarnation. The ankh was a very powerful symbol in Egyptology. Most pictures drawn in that period have ankhs in them. The Pharaohs were buried with this symbol because they believed it would help them in their next life.

Astrology

This is a religious belief that comes from the Babylonians. It teaches that the stars, moon, and sun can influence man's future. *Warning to Parents:* There are three electronic pocket computers for children that promote astrology:

1. Baby-Sitter's Club Electronic Diary
2. Casio Secret Sender 6,000.
3. Dear Diary

The Baby-Sitter's Club Electronic Diary promotional ad reads like this:

Fortune teller—is today going to be a good day for

baby sitting? Ages 5 and up. [I don't know many 5-year-old baby sitters!]

The Casio Secret Sender 6000 promotional ad reads:

> Tells fortunes every day, gives romantic advice. [Recommended ages are 8 and up. Why does an 8-year-old need romantic advice?]

The Dear Diary. One girl told me her friend got a *Dear Diary* for Christmas last year. Now her friend will do nothing without first checking her astrology reading. Both of these little girls come from good Christian homes! Scriptures that refute this are:

> Thou art wearied in the multitude of thy counsels. Let now the astrologers, the stargazers, the monthly prognosticators, stand up, and save thee from these things that shall come upon thee. Behold, they shall be as stubble; the fire shall burn them; they shall not deliver themselves from the power of the flame: there shall not be a coal to warm at, nor fire to sit before it (Isa. 47:13–14).

> Thus saith the LORD, Learn not the way of the heathen, and be not dismayed at the signs of heaven; for the heathen are dismayed at them (Jer. 10:2).

Five-Pointed Star

This symbol, better known as the pentagram, or Baphomet, is used as a power sign in the occult. When one point is up and two points are down, it is the symbol for witchcraft. The five points represent the five elements of witchcraft—earth, wind, fire, water, and spirit. When

Witchcraft

Satanism

the pentagram is upside down, with two points up and one point down, it is a symbol for Satanism. It is called Baphomet. Again, this star represents Satan.

> And the fifth angel sounded, and I saw a star fall from heaven unto the earth: and to him was given the key of the bottomless pit (Rev. 9:1).

Italian Horn

This is supposed to be a lucky charm to bring you finances. I remember speaking in a church service and after my message a girl was brought to me. She was about twenty-one years old. We sat down and talked about the demonic oppression she was having. I noticed that she was wearing an occult symbol on a necklace. It was the leprechaun staff, better known as the Italian horn. I asked her if she knew what it meant. She said, "Yes." She proceeded to tell me that as I was speaking, the horn got so hot she had to lift it away from her neck.

She then told me that sometimes in her dreams the Devil would tell her that she was his because she wore his symbol. After counseling her for about an hour, she gave us the necklace and the pastor threw it away. Do you know where she got this necklace? It was given to her by a boyfriend at her Christian school graduation. She was told by this young man, "Don't ever take this necklace off and you will always know someone loves you." Be very careful when someone gives you something and tells you not to take it off.

If you have the Lord Jesus Christ as your supplier, you don't need the Devil's horn to bring you finances!

Lightning Bolt

This symbol is rightly called the satanic "S." Rock groups like AC/DC use this symbol. It's a symbol of power. The Nazi SS soldiers also used the lightning bolt as a symbol of power and speed. But again, before AC/DC and Hitler, it was a symbol for Satan.

And he [Jesus] said unto them, I beheld Satan as lightning fall from heaven (Luke 10:18).

Ouija Board

According to *Consumer's Report,* the Ouija board was voted the second most popular board game among teens in 1994 (Monopoly won first place). It is played by youth groups at slumber parties, as well as some church activities, but do they know the background behind this seemingly harmless game? The Ouija board is far from being harmless. It was created by the Wiccans as a means for them to communicate with the dead. Again, I must tell you that these people do not talk to the dead. They talk to familiar spirits, which are demons that imitate people. This is no game. The Ouija board is an occult tool that Christians should avoid.

How old is the Ouija board? No one really knows, yet similar occult tools have been traced back to ancient Chinese, Greek, and Egyptian cultures. If you ever have the chance to visit St. Augustine, Florida, you should go. It's a beautiful little town and is known to be the oldest city in America. While there, you might go to the toy shop. The only toys displayed there are from the 1500s, yet above the door you will see a Ouija board nailed to the wall.

William Fuld, of Baltimore, has been credited with the invention of the Ouija board. However, it was patented by Elijah Bond in 1891. The common board as we know it today was patented on May 2, 1939. The Ouija board was very popular in the 1920s when it was reported that 3 million boards had been sold. In the 1960s the revival of the occult brought along with it the increase in demand for the boards. Ownership of William Fuld, Inc. was purchased by Parker Brothers on February 23, 1966, and by the late 1970s sales were reported at 7 million for the decade.[1]

This is not a game and should be taken seriously. Many years ago I was having a question and answer time during Sunday school. We were talking about demonic activities when a lady stood up to share. Her story is not uncommon to those who have tampered with the supernatural via the Ouija board. She said, "Years ago my sister was playing with a Ouija board and it told her that she was going to die. She asked it how, and the board said she was going to be murdered. She asked by whom. It replied, 'Your husband.' On the very date indicated by that board, her husband did kill her."

Maybe you have played with the Ouija board and it told you some things that have left you feeling helpless. That is not necessarily true. If you are a Christian you can reject those sayings, confess your involvement with this board as sin, and ask Jesus Christ to control your future, not a Ouija board.

Peace Sign

Witches foot, or Nero's cross, was made popular in the 1960s and is now having a resurgence in the 1990s. It might have been the well-known humanist, Bertrand Russell, who commissioned Gerald Holton to design this symbol as a rallying sign for leftist marches.

This symbol is the Teutonic rune of death. Some contend that Hitler may have used the symbol on his death warrants. Even though Holton and Russell convinced the masses that this sign was a symbol of peace, nothing could be further from the truth.

Before Holton, before Russell, and before Hitler, there was a man after whom this symbol was named. Perhaps its true meaning lies in the kind of person he was. His name was Nero, an emperor of Rome. No one ever hated Christians as much as he. History tells us that Christians were used as torches to light the streets of Rome. Nero personally had the Apostle Peter crucified. The story is told that Peter did not feel worthy to die in the same position as the Lord Jesus Christ, so he asked to be crucified upside down. It was symbolic of how he came forth from his mother's womb.

A former Satanist recently told me that for his initiation he had to hold a ceramic cross above his head and break it as a sign of his devotion to Satan.

So, one may ask, "Why is it called the peace sign?" During the 1960s, there was a vile spirit of lust, free sex, drugs, and rock and roll. It was the Christians who stood against that movement. Maybe these people felt the world would be a better place, filled with peace, if there were no Christian opposition.

Swastika

If you thought the swastika was created for Hitler's Nazi movement you're wrong. The swastika is an ancient sacred symbol of pagan cultures. The Sanskrit word for swastika means "fortunate," or possibly "good luck." To those who are associated with witchcraft it symbolizes Mother Goddess. It is also known as the solar wheel. The four bends, or hooks, in the cross represent the four directions of the earth.

Yin Yang

An occult belief that teaches universal energies which a person can choose. We, as Christians, do not believe in a force.

We believe in a personal God. God spoke to Moses from a burning bush. The Devil tempted Eve. These are not impersonal "forces." (See my book, *Fourteen Things Witches Hope Parents Never Find Out*, p. 125.)

NEW AGE VS. CHRISTIANITY— A CONTRAST

From "New Age Cults and Religions"

(Reprinted with permission by Texe Marrs[1])

○ **New Age teaching.** "God" is the creation and creator, the All-in-One. He/She/It is the Divine Intelligence and the Creative Force.

Bible teaching. God is separate from, greater than, and Master of His creation (Acts 17:28; Col. 1:16–17; 1 Cor. 4:7; Gen. 1:1, Isa. 48:11–12).

○ **New Age teaching.** God and the Holy Spirit are impersonal: a presence, a vibration, an energy force, universal law, Universal Mind, Cosmic Consciousness, Divine Presence, Eternal Reality, Real Presence, Creative Force, Cosmic One, etc.

Bible teaching. God is "Personal." Though a spirit, He is infinite, eternally transcendent (external to man), and worthy of our worship (John 1; 16:13–14; Rev. 4:11).

○ **New Age teaching.** Each human being is endowed with a spark of divinity. An illumined, or enlightened, person

is beyond such moral distinctions as "good" or "bad."
Bible teaching. Humanity is fallen, born in bondage
to sin, and in need of redemption. Satan is real and evil
exists. Man can become free of the condemnation of sin
through Jesus Christ (Rom. 3:23; John 3:16–19; 8:44;
Jer. 17:5–9; Eph. 2:8–9; Rev. 20).

○ **New Age teaching.** Jesus did not die for the sins of
the world. His shedding of blood, though tragic, is irrel-
evant to man's spiritual needs today. No atonement.
Christianity is a "bloody religion."
Bible teaching. Jesus died on the cross as a sin sacrifice. Through His blood we are saved and through His
resurrection we are assured of eternal life and victory
over death (Heb. 9:22; Matt. 26–28; John 3:16; Rom. 3:23;
Gal. 1:1–5; 2 Cor. 5:21; Eph. 2:8–9).

○ **New Age teaching.** Jesus was a god, a Christ, a perfect Master, a man who earned his divinity, a perfected
man, a prophet of God; He was as much God as are all of
us.
Bible teaching. Jesus is, was, and forever shall be God
Almighty, the one true God; and there is no other besides Him. Jesus created all things. He, the Father, and
the Holy Spirit are eternally One. They cannot be separated—ever. There is but one Godhead. Jesus is the only
Christ (1 John 2:20–25; Heb. 1:8; Col. 1:14–19, 2:9–10).

○ **New Age teaching.** Man must take responsibility for
his problems and forgive himself. There is no one outside of man to whom we must plead for forgiveness, no
one outside of ourselves who can forgive us.
Bible teaching. A loving God can forgive our sins and
cleanse us. He offers man the free gift of salvation (1
Pet. 1; 1 John 1:2–6, 3:16; James 4:6–11).

○ **New Age teaching.** Man must endure many life cycles (reincarnation) until his karma is cleansed, pure spirit is achieved, and union with "God" attained.

Bible teaching. Man has only one physical life on earth. Upon death, man returns to God, the Creator, who is our Judge. Those saved escape condemnation and receive eternal life (John 3:16; Heb. 9:27).

○ **New Age teaching.** Through good works and/or enlightenment, man can aspire to divinity and union with "God" (all that is). This is the universal law.

Bible teaching. Man is not saved by law or through his good works. Nor can man become enlightened through his own efforts. Eternal life and Heaven are free gifts given by a loving, personal God to those who accept His grace and are thus born again (Gal. 3:1–4, 2:16; Titus 3:5; John 3:3).

○ **New Age teaching.** Eating meat produces negative karma in a person. Meat is forbidden and the (enlightened) superior spiritual being does not eat meat (vegetarianism).

Bible teaching. God blesses all things He has created for man to eat, including meat (Col 2:16; 1 Tim. 4:3).

○ **New Age teaching.** Spirit beings, or entities, are able to provide spiritual insight and guidance. They are helpers who can show man how to become fully conscious and realize self (become divine).

Bible teaching. There is only one mediator between man and God—Christ Jesus. Communication with spirit guides and entities is an occult practice called necromancy. It is an abomination to God. Such spirits are unclean and not of God (Deut. 18:10–12; 1 Tim. 4:1; Isa. 8:19; 1 Sam. 28:1–25; 1 Chr. 10:13–14).

○ **New Age teaching.** The Holy Bible is insufficient as a guide for man. Other "bibles" from other religions, ancient religious texts and writings, and fresh new revelations either from people living today or spirit entities are equally as valuable and reliable.

Bible teaching. The Bible is authoritative, powerful, and able to guide man in every aspect of his life, producing joy and satisfaction in the reader who knows Christ as Lord (Rev. 22:18–19; John 5:39; Acts 17:2, 11, 18:28; Rom. 15:4, 16:26; 2 Pet. 1:21).

○ **New Age teaching.** Man is part of and one with the creation; the creation is "God," thus man is also "God." He is co-creator of the universe. Through an evolutionary process, man is "awakening" and returning to godhood.

Bible teaching. God is the great I AM—transcendent to His creation, magnificent, glorious, King of kings. Man is made to serve God. Someday, every knee will bow and every tongue confess that Jesus Christ is Lord (Phil. 5:2–13; Rev. 22:18–19; John 5:39; Rev. 21:1–8, 22:8–9; Matt. 18:3; John 3:3, 14:6).

Recommended Reading from the Book Shelf

New Age Cults and Religions, Texe Marrs
Straight Answers On the New Age, Bob Larson
Psychic Forces and Occult Shock, John Weldon and Clifford
 Wilson
When the World Will Be As One, Tal Brooke
Apologetics In the New Age, David K. Clark and Norman
 L. Geisler

Section IV

ENCOURAGEMENT FOR THE CHRISTIAN

DUNGEON/ & DRAGON/— ARE ROLE PLAYING GAME/ PO/ITIVE?

Personal Testimony of Jerry Smith, Jr.

Sometime in the early 1970s, a new type of game began to sweep the nation and even the world. This new form of entertainment, known as role-playing, allowed ordinary people to escape the pressures and confinements of society and indulge in their fantasies to be powerful adventurers encountering and conquering great adversaries. In the realm of role-playing, anything is possible; it is a splendid dimension where dreams are fulfilled and wishes come true.

Role-playing is a mental game that requires imagination. The more imagination one has, the more realistic and enjoyable the game is. One begins by creating the character that he will role-play and detailing the personality, history, and traits of his Player Character (PC for short). The character has defined skills, abilities, intelligence, strength, social position, appearance, occupation, and class. Upon completion of these preliminaries, several individuals meet and integrate their PCs into a party and submit this party to the referee of the game, or Game Master (more commonly referred to as the Dungeon Master, or DM). The DM then narrates everything that the PCs encounter and controls the actions and events.

The DM is an experienced player, usually with several years of play, and has a great deal of understanding as to the mechanics of the game. Although the game is relatively simple for the players (having only to be concerned with the actions of their PCs), the DM must oversee and control every aspect of the game from the weather, the passing of time (a difficult task governing exhaustion, hunger, etc.), the people encountered on a journey, and especially battles between the party and outside characters (these outside characters are Non-Player Characters, or NPCs, and are everything from the simple barmaid to a giant dragon). The ruling of the DM is final in all cases and is indisputable. In essence, the DM is the virtual omniscient, omnipresent, and all-powerful god of the realm.

An important thing to know is that a great deal of preparation must go into every campaign (a group of related adventures). For every hour of play, two or more hours go into preparation for the game to ensure good organization. Much more time is necessary for the design of adventures, castles, countries, and dungeons.

I was first introduced to role-playing halfway through my seventh grade year. A friend of mine was new to the popular game Dungeons & Dragons (D&D for short). We both began to play slowly, learning the rules as we went along and taking turns as DM while the other was the PC. Toward the end of seventh grade I began to read the rule books and study the various monsters and classes of characters (the character class is the major role of the PC: a fighter, thief, magic-user, etc.). My parents, thrilled with the fact that I had voluntarily read anything, bought me D&D materials.

I expanded my vocabulary and knowledge of ancient mythology through the extensive reading required to fully grasp the rules and concepts of the game. I became more creative and imaginative as my PCs faced different trials and difficulties in their adventures. All seemed to be well.

All was not well, however. The study required a great amount of time and energy. At the end of the summer, I had lost interest in most of the other activities I used to enjoy. My days were filled with preparation for playing D&D. When eighth grade had begun, I was spending seven or more hours a day on the game. School interfered with my time to play D&D; I no longer had the vast amounts of time for preparation I had during the summer. To compensate, my friends and I began to play D&D during school. At first, we played at lunch and PE, but as time progressed we began to prepare for the game and eventually play the game during classes. My group would even play over the phone late at night.

As a result, my grades began to drop as my involvement with the game increased. I spent little or no time on homework and concentrated on the game. My parents assumed that I was studying school work because I was always quiet and in my room. My attitude toward school and others began to take a turn for the worst. I viewed school as a pointless waste of time and had no qualms with brazenly announcing this fact to my instructors. We lost our respect and fear of authority and began to leave school during lunch to eat off campus (our school was a small private school of approximately 300 students and about half a mile from a mall). My thoughts had become consumed with the game. I began to spend a large amount of money to build up my library of books on D&D—more money than I had. I began to get money any way I could to buy books and new adventure modules. My grades plummeted and I still wonder how I passed my Algebra I course. Toward the end of my eighth grade year, several others in my group and I were caught painting graffiti inside the gymnasium. I had worn out my welcome at that school.

I continued to play during the summer, mostly with my younger brother, as I prepared to change schools and attend the larger public high school. I had little contact with my old D&D friends since I had changed schools and so my play was not as intense. My grades were good; I had a strong B average in all my studies. After about four months, I began to meet others at my high school who were interested in D&D and I introduced the game to a few friends who had never played before. As my new group grew, I returned to my habit of time-consuming preparation for the game, thus my grades began to fall again as I slowly reverted to the individual I had been only a year before.

That summer, I continually met with friends to play D&D. We would spend the weekend at each other's houses to play the game. By tenth grade, our group was in full swing as we played and prepared every moment we could. We skipped PE to play D&D.

The individuals in our group came from different backgrounds but most of us were either intellectuals or troublemakers; I tended to be a member of the latter. Despite our differences, we developed over-zealous loyalties toward one another. Our loyalties, however, depended on the events in our character's lives. If anyone's character opposed my PC, then I began to hate them as if they were against me. Invisible cliques began to divide our loyalties as our PCs, and eventually ourselves, plotted vengeance on other PCs and people.

I subtly began to lose distinctions between what was the game and what was reality. This was a growing problem; my characters were usually thieves. As I would progress through the day, I attempted to react as my character and looked for opportunities to be a thief. My mind was set on putting myself within the game to have a more exciting time. I became more aggressive and sought out opportunities to fight. I even followed an individual for several days with whom I had had a confrontation, antagonizing him into fighting me. My character had begun to overtake me; better still, my darker side began to dominate my life.

With these changes in attitude from an easy-going individual to an aggressive teen, I lost my fear and respect for authority. I began to skip classes and whole school days. We became so brazen that we would even walk off campus while teachers watched us. I missed so many days in my Spanish and English classes, I should have failed. Once we were stopped by a police officer while leaving campus and brazenly lied to him. Eventually we were caught once skipping class. As a result, we received three days suspension pending a conference between our parents and the principal. I was so bold as to call the principal who had suspended me, and impersonate my father on the phone so that I could return to school the next day. Through a strange twist of events, my parents discovered that I had been suspended and when inquiring from the school as to my whereabouts, the discrepancy was noticed. The school officials called me into the office with my parents to discuss the situation. I could not be punished twice for skipping class, so the three-day suspension was converted to three licks, and I found my first loophole. I was to go unpunished; however, unknown to me until later, my father wanted me to receive a form of punishment from the school in an attempt to show me their authority. The result was one week of In School Suspension (ISS).

ISS didn't bother me. Honestly, I preferred the solitude to the boring lectures of teachers. I quickly finished a week's worth of assignments in a day and a half. However, I was smart enough to pretend that it took me the rest of the week to finish my Algebra II work, otherwise I would have done a stupid report on the aardvark.

I began to look for other loopholes in the rules as I tried to place myself in more situations like my character. I began to drink socially and periodically at the age of fifteen. I began to think of running away so I could live on the streets like my thieves would. I thought of what I would have to do to survive—steal, swindle, or worse. I often thought of death. Within the game, there is a great deal of death and violence. I contemplated my own demise in the game and in reality, as well as the death of people I knew. I began to wonder what it would feel like to be like my thief and murder someone for no reason other than the fact that I possessed the power to do so. More and more my thoughts turned to illegal activities and I conceived well-planned activities.

I began to neglect my family and grew further from my parents and brother. This continued throughout the summer. I had left a few of my gaming friends because of the dissension within the original group. I spent hours planning campaigns and began to fail the course I took in summer school.

I began to play with a group more as fall semester began. My problems worsened; I was grossly insubordinate with all school officials and would argue whenever antagonized. I continued to drink socially and began to smoke. I found several other loopholes in the rules and continued to get into trouble as I debated the semantics of the rule book.

My parents were concerned with my changes over the past several years. They first thought it was just a stage I was progressing through. They eventually realized that there was a connection to the friends I had and tried to keep me apart from the group. They soon discovered that this was not the real reason. It had little to do with my friends but everything to do with the game. Finally accepting this fact, they collected everything I had on D&D and destroyed it all before I could stop them.

Several months later I began to accept that my parents would not allow me to have anything to do with the game. I began to find new friends; my old ones could not play with me any longer and I feared what my parents would do if they found out I was still gaming (there was talk of military school). My grades began to increase and in my senior year I had perfect attendance and a straight A average. I even made a 5 on the AP Calculus exam the following spring.

As my involvement with D&D progressed, I lost interest in all other activities. I lost respect for authority and became more difficult to control. I became increasingly paranoid in the tenth grade, fearing my fellow players who opposed me. I felt as though every school official was against me and tried to antagonize me. The game became my life and it consumed my thoughts and time. I did very little school work in the tenth grade, and as a result my scores fell. I began to think that my life was a game, and did not realize the consequences of what I was doing. I forgot that I could not take back any action I did in reality as I could in the game.

As my characters matured, they became more ruthless, committing heinous crimes ranging from rape and torture to cold-blooded and disgusting murder. They had no shame. What if I had lost all sight of reality and allowed myself to be completely consumed in the game and began to live even more like my characters? I would now be either in jail or dead.

Role-playing games are exciting to participate in. I still miss playing and still contemplate joining a group. However, I remember how addictive they are and how they consumed me and changed me. I never want to be in that state of mind again. The game altered my thoughts and actions to those which are not acceptable within our society.

TERMS AND DEFINITIONS RELATING TO DUNGEONS & DRAGONS

Note. "Playing" means not only direct and immediate participation in the role-playing aspects of the game, but also any preparation and study for direct role-playing.

Note. "ISS" In School Suspension—a disciplinary action in which students attend a different school to study and continually work in a boot-camp fashion; every aspect of daily life is controlled in ISS.

Note. "Officials" refers to anyone with governing authority, be it the school principle, law officer, or disciplinary officials of ISS.

D&D. Dungeons & Dragons—the first and most popular role-playing game.

AD&D. Advanced D&D—an advanced version; the PCs and DMs have more liberty and control over the rules.

DM. Dungeon Master—the referee or director of the game; his word is the ultimate rule over all aspects of the game.

PC. Player Character—the imaginary character an individual controls and directs.

NPC. Non-Player Character—character in the game that is controlled by the Dungeon Master.

Class. The major adventuring role of the PC—in order of frequency: Fighter, Magic-User, Cleric, Thief, Barbarian, Acrobat, Cavilier, Ranger, Paladin, Druid, Illusionist, Bard, Assassin.

> **Fighter.** A strong warrior (self-explanatory).
>
> **Magic-User.** Wizard—has a variety of spells for many different situations.
>
> **Cleric.** A holy man or priest who has fighting capabilities and healing powers.
>
> **Thief.** A regular, all-around thief (self-explanatory).
>
> **Barbarian.** An uncivilized fighter from a tribal clan.
>
> **Acrobat.** A thief which specializes in cat-burglary.
>
> **Cavilier.** A noble warrior or knight.
>
> **Ranger.** A tracker, scout, and fighter.
>
> **Paladin.** A crusading warrior.
>
> **Druid.** A member of a religious sect with ability to call on nature's powers.
>
> **Illusionist.** A wizard who specializes in deceiving the senses.
>
> **Bard.** An experienced fighter and thief who develops spells and has the profession of a minstrel.
>
> **Assassin.** A thief who specializes in murder (self-explanatory).

Party. A collection of unified PCs and NPCs.

Realm. The universe in which all PCs and NPCs exist.

Modules. Store-bought campaigns or adventures.

Campaign. A group or series of related adventures which could last from several months to years in "game time."

Game Time. The point in time where the PCs and NPCs are. The clock runs during play at a rate dependent on the actions of the PCs and NPCs.

TIME LINE OF MY PROGREJJION/DIGREJJION INTO D&D

I. Introduction to Game
A. What is Role-Playing: basic principles
B. How does it work: rules, DM

II. My Experience
A. Beginnings mid-7th grade
1. Benefits
2. Mom and Dad liked

B. The 8th Grade
1. School—no desire, pointless
2. School—played during class
3. School—grades dropped
4. Changes in attitude
5. Began to skip school
6. Spent great deal of money:
   a. Got money anyway I could
   b. No respect for the value of money
7. Confrontations with school officials

8. Thought of game constantly—consumed my time and thoughts

C. 9th Grade—Change of Schools

1. New school—found friends to play with after about four months
2. Acquainted others to game or got others more involved
3. Grades began strong but decreased as I found friends with which to play
4. Began to spend great deal of time preparing as the group became more organized

D. 10th Grade—Grades Worsened

1. Group was in full swing
   a. Mostly intellectuals or social derelicts
   b. Spent nights and weekends together playing
2. Group grew very close
   a. Developed over-zealous loyalties to others
   b. Began to hate anyone who would oppose my character in a game
   c. Plotted revenge against characters, and eventually individuals
3. Began to always think as if I were a character in the game
   a. Thief
   b. Look for opportunities for revenge—fight with J. T.
4. Gross insubordination—loss of respect for authority
   a. Began to skip school—brazenly
      i. Should have failed—I missed so many days
      ii. Stopped by officer once and lied to him
   b. ISS situation with lying to principal
   c. Looked for rules to break

5. Illegal activity
   a. Sought anything that could put me in a real-life situation like my game character
   b. Began to drink periodically and socially
   c. Thought of death
      i. My death
      ii. Death of others
      iii. Murder of others
6. Actively thought of ways to break law

E. 11th Grade
   1. Problems worsened
   2. Continued to associate with old D&D friends
   3. Drinking and smoking periodically and socially—"controlled substances"
   4. Confrontation with school officials—arguing the rules
      a. Searched for loopholes—food on campus
      b. Argues semantics
   5. Parents began to realize the cause of these negative changes
   6. Parents took away everything related to D&D

III. Effects of D&D
   A. Lack of respect for others and authority
   B. Consumed time, money, and thoughts
   C. Heinous crimes of my characters
   D. Loss of self identity and began to lose sight of reality—paranoia with teachers and officials.

A PARENTS' GUIDE TO SELECTING CHILDREN'S TV PROGRAMS

The problem with writing a book dealing with children's television programs is that they run their course in popularity. After a few years they lose their marketability. Book sales may drop, but the media continues to move ahead with new programs that will further indoctrinate your children. I hope that this segment of the book will be of value to you, as a parent, for years to come.

There are seven major themes that may be harmful to your child's emotional and spiritual development. A rating system is given here for you to use.

1. Violence. This can be divided into two types:
   a. Mild. Slapstick violence where bodily harm does not occur, or where there is minimal property damage.
   b. Extreme. Something to cause concern for parents.

2. Evolutionist mutations. The only way evolution can explain its theory is through the mutation process which teaches that a mutation can evolve to a superior species.

Evolutionists would find themselves hard pressed to give one scientific example of this process. If mutations could evolve into a superior species, why don't we find mutated things evolving today?

So humanism does what science cannot do—it creates superheroes out of mutations (Teenage Mutant Ninja Turtles, X-Men, Fantastic Four, etc.)

> In the beginning God created the heaven and the earth. . . . And God said, Let us make man in our image, after our likeness: and let them have dominion over the fish of the sea, and over the fowl of the air, and over the cattle, and over all the earth, and over every creeping thing that creepeth upon the earth. . . . And God blessed them, and God said unto them, Be fruitful, and multiply, and replenish the earth, and subdue it . . . (Gen. 1:1,26,28)

Barney recently had a birthday party. The girl told Barney that she was sorry she could not put 200 million candles on the cake. Evolution is being subtly dropped on your children. (For more information on Barney, see my book entitled *Fourteen Things Witches Hope Parents Never Find Out*.)[1]

3. Goddess worship. Today, feminists and witches are attacking the fact that God is a male gender. There is a new Bible on the market that refers to His/Her, or Our Mother/Father, which art in heaven. Mainline denominations are accepting Sophia as a substitute for Jesus Christ! (Examples of this are found in *Captain Planet*.)

4. Supernaturals.
    a. Elementals. The elementals in witchcraft are earth, wind, fire, water, and spirit (as in *Captain Planet, Pocahontas,* and others).

b. **Sorcery, wizards, and magic.** The use of supernatural power (as in *Smurfs, Sorcerer's Apprentice, Care Bears,* and others).

c. **Spirits.** Supernatural beings that are supposed to intervene on behalf of mortals (as in *Ghost, Casper,* Grandmother Willow in *Pocahontas, Ghost Busters,* Dare Devil from *Fantastic 4*). This last character has a red suit complete with horns and a tail, yet he represents good.

d. **Power items.** Such as wands, crystals, pyramids, trolls, pentagrams, etc. (Power Rangers).

e. **Meditation.** This is altered states of consciousness (Rafiki in *The Lion King*).

5. **New Age doctrines.**

a. **Reincarnation.** Examples of reincarnation can be found in *The Lion King, Casper, Pocahontas* (see "New Age Terms").

b. **Telepathy, or psychic powers.** The ability to communicate with someone by mental powers. For example, in the movie *Teenage Mutant Ninja Turtles,* Leonardo contacts Splinter. Rafiki, in *The Lion King,* knew that Simba was alive. Captain Planet is another example.

c. **Visualization.** This has to do with bringing your thoughts into reality by way of meditation. For example, Barney is an imaginary problem-solver. New Agers would call him a spirit guide.

6. **Rejection of authority.** Bart Simpson, G.I. Joe, Beavis and Butthead.

7. **Martial arts.** This needs a little explaining. If martial arts is used for self-defense it's all right. However, many cartoons and programs use it as a means of teaching medi-

tation, telepathy, and other occult practices. Many young people are joining martial arts classes because of Power Rangers, Teenage Mutant Ninja Turtles, only to find out it is a breeding ground for Buddhism.

CHECK LIST FOR PARENTS

Name of Cartoon: _____

Does this program expose my child to:

[ ] Violence?   [ ] Goddess Worship?
   [ ] Mild   [ ] Extreme   [ ] Supernaturals?
[ ] Martial Arts?   [ ] New Age Doctrine?
[ ] Evolution/Mutations?   [ ] Rejection of Authority?

Questions to Consider
Based On Program Content

Will this program: **Yes**   **No**

O de-sensitize my child to things which are   [ ]   [ ]
   bad?

O promote values that are contrary to the   [ ]   [ ]
   Word of God?

O become a tool for a New Age teacher to   [ ]   [ ]
   teach my child occultism?

O undermine my authority as a parent?   [ ]   [ ]

WHO WILL FILL THE GAP?

When was the last time you heard the term, "generation gap"? In the 1960s and '70s we were told that this gap separated the children's lives from the lives of their parents. Parenting experts told parents not to spank children. They were encouraged to be a friend to their children. To treat the children in an adult fashion. Now we no longer have parents, we have friends. We no longer have a gap, we have a humanistic bridge.

What was so wrong with parents in the 1960s and '70s? As far as I can tell, God intended that parents would bring stability into the home. Now, in the 1990s, the home is in shambles. Again we see how Satan deliberately reverses God's rules so he can cause chaos. God's plan is that children would go through adolescence so that, when they themselves became parents, they would be able to help their children get through adolescence. Today the parents are caught in adolescence alongside the child. Let me illustrate this point.

Rock music used to be only a teen problem. Now parents, who were teenagers in the 1960s and '70s, listen to the same rock music as their kids. These parents had the Stones, the Eagles, Grateful Dead, the Beatles, etc. Some of these groups are now on tour drawing parents and children alike. Today you find parents smoking marijuana with their children. You find that weekend drunken parties are now thrown by adults.

For most, adolescence is generally the hardest time in life. It's a time when young people try to find out who they are and where they are going in life. God provided a "gap" between childhood and adulthood so that parents could help pull children out of adolescence. Because our society listened to the humanist, we now find that parents themselves are trapped in an adolescence of their own because no one was there to pull them out. Now that the divorce rate is near 50 percent, this has catapulted parents back into the dating scene again. The major cause of divorce is that of unresolved problems in adolescence. Let me explain.

We know that teenagers from the 1960s and '70s were taught to have sex at a young age. So they became sexually active in their early teens. During this time they would have many different partners between thirteen and twenty years of age. Then they would get married, which is supposed to be one partner for a lifetime. However, a few months later they became unfaithful. Divorce followed.

Please don't misunderstand me. I am not trying to put single parents on a guilt trip, nor am I trying to make victims of divorce second-class citizens. Our churches are filled with loving, caring people who were victims, not culprits. One of the fastest growing ministries today is the single ministry. The church needs to help stabilize those who have been wounded by the world.

My point is that God put a gap between children and parents for a purpose. And it's a "gap," not a great fixed gulf. Children will have many friends in their lifetime, but they have only one set of biological parents. Here is the key to this chapter: When Satan removed the gap he removed the authority. Satan has always known that if you remove the authority you have no rules. If you have no rules you have no guidelines. If you have no guidelines you have confusion. And Satan is the author of confusion. No matter what the world tells you, the Word of God says:

Train up a child in the way he should go: and when he is old, he will not depart from it (Prov. 22:6.).

OVERCOMING FEAR BY FAITH

Fear is one of the oldest weapons in Satan's arsenal, yet by no means is it obsolete. Without a doubt, it's one of his most powerful and destructive weapons. It's a weapon that causes massive destruction, and yet has pinpoint accuracy. Fear, to Satan's army, is what the Tomahawk missile is to ours. Once the Tomahawk missile locks onto its programmed target, it will avoid all other obstacles to hit it. Fear is just the same. Once fear locks in on us it will bypass all of our strengths and target our one weakest area.

Many people today confuse the words "fear" and "afraid." They are not words with the same meaning. I fear the Lord, or in other words, I reverence and worship Him because of His awesome powers, and for the fact that He is God and is greater than anything. We should never be afraid of God. He has only our best interests in mind.

For I know the thoughts that I think toward you, saith the Lord, thoughts of peace, and not of evil, to give you an expected end. Then shall ye call upon me, and ye shall go and pray unto me, and I will hearken unto you. And ye shall seek me, and find me, when ye shall search for me with all your heart. And I will be found of you, saith the Lord: and I will turn away your captivity (Jer. 29:11–14).

On the other hand, Satan does not have our best interests at heart. People are afraid of the Devil because of what he might do to them. He means to hurt us.

A good example of this would be when we warn our children about things that may hurt them—like playing in a busy street, or touching a hot stove. As they get older, we warn them about drugs and alcohol. We want them to fear because we love them and don't want them to get hurt. Sometimes we even have to discipline them for disobeying our warning. Fear is a good thing when it protects us.

Satan's fear is intended to put us into captivity and bondage to him. The fear of God is designed to free us.

Satan may use the things listed in Romans 8:35 to make us fearful: tribulation, distress, persecution, famine, nakedness, peril, or the sword. But God says in verses 38–39 that we don't have to fear these things because nothing can separate us from the love of God. Plus, He also gives us assurance in Romans 8:31, "What shall we then say to these things? If God be for us, who can be against us?"

Here are a few specific ways Satan will use fear:

Uncertainties About the Future Will Cause Fear

Several years ago I experienced a fury of fear. It came during a transition in my life. My family and I had been on the road for five years. We were living in a 42-foot fifth-wheel trailer, traveling from town to town holding meetings. My wife and I decided it was time for us to get off the road and enroll our children in a good Christian school. They were eight and ten years of age at the time.

We tried to buy a home near the church and school but our income was insufficient and would not allow us to do this. The part of town we wanted to live in had very few rentals, so for several months we lived in a campground about 25 miles away from the church. Well, winter was setting in and the owner notified us that we would have to vacate the premises. There was no other campground open in the area so we had to store our trailer and move into a hotel. It was while we were living in this hotel that I had a tremendous battle with fear.

I can understand why people with phobias can crawl into a corner and shake uncontrollably. It is estimated that 50 percent of all mental cases deal with fear. Without a caring, loving wife, two wonderful God-sent children, and the precious Holy Spirit of God I, too, could have very easily ended up in the hospital. That was several years ago, and yet tears still fill my eyes as I write about it.

Here is how Satan used fear to attack me. He put a thought in my mind that I was going to die. I woke up one night and looked at my two children lying fast asleep without a care in the world. My wife was resting confidently next to me knowing that everything was going to be all right. It was then that I thought I was going to die. I didn't hear an audible voice but Satan used my thoughts. He said, "David, look around you. You have worked for God all these years and you only have a motel room for your family. You're going to die and all your family will have is a motel room."

He continued, "David, you're not saved because if you were God's child and you did all of this in His name, you wouldn't be here." My friend, I got out of that bed and cried out to God. I wanted to know if I really was God's child. I went to the Word of God and as I turned the pages it seemed like there was a verse on every page assuring me that I was His child.

No, I wasn't healed of fear instantly. This battle went on for several months. It was Christmas time, which only added to the dilemma because it seemed like everyone should have a home to spend Christmas in. I can't tell you the exact day or hour when fear left, but I can tell you that it didn't leave until I took authority over it by using the Word of God. You see, faith cometh by hearing, and hearing by the Word of God (Rom. 10:17).

By the way, the Lord miraculously used a man named Tom and a lady named Lois, very dear friends of ours, to help us get into a house. God is good!

Fear Motivated by Guilt

Several weeks ago a young lady called my office. She was doubting her salvation. Not only was she doubting her salvation, she also believed that she had passed the point of forgiveness, feeling that she had committed the unpardonable sin. I could tell by her voice that she was very disturbed about her condition.

My curiosity was running wild—just like yours is right now! I had to ask her what sins she had committed that would drive her to such fear and guilt. Was it Satanism? Had she joined a group that made her swear against God? No! Was she involved with witchcraft and tormented by demonic spirits? No! Maybe she was a prostitute or drug addict? No! Could it be that she had killed someone and the memory was haunting her? No! All of these things were going through my mind. I said, "Tell me what horrible sin you have committed." She paused, hesitated for a moment, and then told me this story:

"Well, Mr. Benoit, several years ago a friend of mine asked me to fast and pray with her about a specific need she had. We were supposed to do this for two days. After the first day I had to eat. I broke a vow, Mr. Benoit, and now I can't be saved."

Some of you may think this is a strange story but it's not. Satan will get you to doubt your salvation and torment you with fear. I'm not talking about losing your salvation. I'm not talking about eternal security. I'm talking about being tormented. Many people come to me about this very issue. "Am I saved or am I lost?" This is their question. When counseling people with this problem I gener-

ally ask, "How long have you doubted your salvation?" The
answer is the same almost every time. "I've doubted my
salvation ever since I've been saved." To that I respond,
"You see, before you are saved the Devil tells you you're
not so bad. Do you know why? Because he knows no one is
good enough to go to heaven."

> For by grace are ye saved through faith; and that not
> of yourselves: it is the gift of God: Not of works, lest any
> man should boast (Eph. 2:8–9).

Satan would never tell a lost person he's not saved for
fear he would get saved. Telling a lost person he isn't saved
brings conviction, and that's the role of the Holy Spirit.
Satan's role is to condemn the saints, not to convict sinners. He is called the accuser of the brethren.

> And I heard a loud voice saying in heaven, Now is
> come salvation, and strength, and the kingdom of our
> God, and the power of his Christ: for the accuser of our
> brethren is cast down, which accused them before our
> God day and night (Rev. 12:10).

You see, if you're not saved the Holy Spirit speaks to
you in a still, small voice and not only tells you that you
need to be saved, but He also tells you how to be saved.
The Devil accuses you and gives you no hope for salvation.
Yes, we have all sinned and come short of the glory of God:

> But God commendeth his love toward us, in that,
> while we were yet sinners, Christ died for us (Rom. 5:8).

Maybe you're wondering why Satan does this. The answer is easy. If you are constantly plagued with fear and
guilt, you will not have the joy of your salvation.

> Now the God of hope fill you with all joy and peace in believing, that ye may abound in hope, through the power of the Holy Ghost (Rom. 15:13).

Satan does not want us to finish our course with joy.

> But none of these things move me, neither count I my life dear unto myself, so that I might finish my course with joy, and the ministry, which I have received of the Lord Jesus, to testify the gospel of the grace of God (Acts 20:24).

Fear Comes When You Want to Serve Christ

I have preached thousands of messages in my lifetime. I've spoken to millions of people via television and radio, yet many times I have fears that I will not remember my message. You must understand, if the Devil cannot get you to doubt God's ability to save you, he will get you to doubt your ability to serve the Lord. There are many people out there in the world who have beautiful voices, yet they never use them for God because of fear. There are many times when people have fears about soul-winning and about giving. Satan will use fear to silence your ministry.

> And I was afraid, and went and hid thy talent in the earth . . . (Matt. 25:25).

Power Verses for Overcoming Fear

Prayerfully read through these questions and meditate on the scriptural answers for each one, giving special attention to the areas that are of concern to your own life. Hopefully you will want to memorize those verses. The Word that you hide in your heart will not only set you free and strengthen you, it will also help you to stand your ground as you speak it out loud when fear tries to defeat you again. Proverbs 18:21 says that death and life are in the power of the tongue, so let your words build a hedge of protection around you.

Remember, every child of God is in a spiritual battle with the enemy. The shield of faith and the sword of the Spirit, which is the Word of God, are part of your spiritual armor and should always be in place so you won't become a casualty.

○ Should we fear our enemies?

I will not be afraid of ten thousands of people, that have set themselves against me round about. Arise, O LORD; save me, O my God: for thou hast smitten all mine enemies upon the cheek bone; thou hast broken the teeth of the ungodly (Ps. 3:6–7).

The LORD is my light and my salvation; whom shall I fear? the LORD is the strength of my life; of whom shall I be afraid? (Ps. 27:1).

The LORD is on my side; I will not fear: what can man do unto me? (Ps. 118:6).

○ Can I sleep, fully confident that God is in control?

When thou liest down, thou shalt not be afraid: yea, thou shalt lie down, and thy sleep shall be sweet. Be not afraid of sudden fear, neither of the desolation of the wicked, when it cometh. For the LORD shall be thy confidence, and shall keep thy foot from being taken (Prov. 3:24–26).

○ What will the fear of man bring?

The fear of man bringeth a snare: but whoso putteth his trust in the LORD shall be safe (Prov. 29:25).

○ What does the Bible mean when it says to "fear" the Lord?

The fear of the LORD is the instruction of wisdom; and before honour is humility (Prov. 15:33).

○ Should we fear the false gods of the New Age?

They [the idols] are upright as the palm tree, but speak not: they must needs be borne [carried], because they cannot go. Be not afraid of them; for they cannot do evil, neither also is it in them to do good. . . . But the LORD is the true God, he is the living God, and an everlasting king (Jer. 10:5, 10).

The gods that have not made the heavens and the earth, even they shall perish from the earth, and from under these heavens (Jer. 10:11).

○ What will God do if we trust Him?

Fear thou not; for I am with thee: be not dismayed; for I am thy God: I will strengthen thee; yea, I will help thee; yea, I will uphold thee with the right hand of my righteousness (Isa. 41:10).

○ Can God give us power over death and the Devil through Jesus Christ?

Forasmuch then as the children are partakers of flesh and blood, he also himself likewise took part of the same; that through death he might destroy him that had the power of death, that is, the devil; And deliver them who through fear of death were all their lifetime subject to bondage (Heb. 2:14–15).

Other Great Verses to Use in Spiritual Warfare

But my God shall supply all your need according to his riches in glory by Christ Jesus (Phil. 4:19).

There is no fear in love; but perfect love casteth out fear: because fear hath torment. He that feareth is not made perfect in love (1 John 4:18).

And he said, The things which are impossible with men are possible with God (Luke 18:27).

I can do all things through Christ which strengtheneth me (Phil. 4:13).

For I have heard the slander of many: fear was on every side: while they took counsel together against me, they devised to take away my life. But I trusted in thee, O LORD: I said, Thou art my God (Ps. 31:13–14).

Wherefore we receiving a kingdom which cannot be moved, let us have grace, whereby we may serve God acceptably with reverence and godly fear (Heb. 12:28).

So that we may boldly say, The Lord is my helper, and I will not fear what man shall do unto me (Heb. 13:6).

Ye are of God, little children, and have overcome them: because greater is he that is in you, than he that is in the world (1 John 4:4, my life verse).

PREPARING THE HOME FOR
SPIRITUAL WARFARE

The home was the first institution established by God, and once the home was established Satan didn't wait very long before he launched his attack against it.

The Attack Against the First Family
In Genesis 3 we read how the Devil tempted Eve into eating the fruit. After the sin came guilt. And after guilt came fear:

> And he said, I heard thy voice in the garden, and I was afraid, because I was naked; and I hid myself (Gen. 3:10).

And after fear came blame:

> And he said, Who told thee that thou wast naked? Hast thou eaten of the tree, whereof I commanded thee that thou shouldest not eat? And the man said, The woman whom thou gavest to be with me, she gave me of the tree, and I did eat (Gen. 3:11–12).

Yes, man blamed the woman and the woman blamed

the serpent and the serpent was speechless and hit the dirt. Blame is possibly one of the most common problems in marriage. It always seems to be the other person's fault.

The Enemy

Finally, my brethren, be strong in the Lord, and in the power of his might. Put on the whole armour of God, that ye may be able to stand against the wiles of the devil. For we wrestle not against flesh and blood, but against principalities, against powers, against the rulers of the darkness of this world, against spiritual wickedness in high places (Eph. 6:10–12).

I used to ask people in fundamental Bible-believing churches if they believed that demonic forces were at work today. Only 50 percent raised their hands. That means that one-half of the congregation didn't even believe they have an enemy. The Bible tells us that we wrestle not against flesh and blood. So if we're not wrestling with flesh and blood, what are we wrestling with? The answer is demonic forces.

If you do not believe you have an enemy you will not defend yourselves. Here is an example. America today is in a dangerous position. She has bought the lie that communism is dead. Now that there is no enemy, we disarm ourselves. I do not believe for one minute that communism is dead. In the same way the Soviets have convinced America they are no longer a threat, the Devil has convinced Christians that demonic forces are no longer a threat. What happens when you don't feel you have an enemy? You disarm yourselves, which is exactly what Christians have done.

Satan's dedication to destroying your home today is the same as it was in the garden with Adam and Eve. Ephesians 6:13 tells us that the activity of demonic forces will only intensify in the evil days. "Wherefore take unto you the whole armour of God, that ye may be able to withstand in the evil day, and having done all, to stand." There is no doubt that we are living in evil days, so this is not the time to put our armor down.

We Need to Dress For a War and Not a Parade

Like most people, I like to go to parades. I enjoy listening to the bands and watching the floats. Many parades have military personnel marching in perfect order, dressed in their finest uniforms. This is the image we have of the military. Yet, when in combat they wear a different uniform. It's a combat uniform, not a parade uniform. Most Christians today are dressed in their parade uniforms, not their combat fatigues. We need to realize that we are not playing war, we're in it! This is not a mock war, nor a war game. The casualties are real. Christians need to be ready to fight the Devil in order to defend our families.

The Bible says, "Be sober [that means get serious], be vigilant; because your adversary the devil, as a roaring lion, walketh about, seeking whom he may devour"(1 Pet. 5:8). When the lion roars in the jungle it causes the adult animals to flee, leaving their young for easy prey. The water buffalo doesn't do that. When adult water buffalo hear the roar of the lion they surround their calves, making it impossible for the lion to kill them. As Christians, we should not be filled with fear and run, leaving our children as prey. We need to surround them with the Word of God and with godly influences in order to ward off the Devil.

Dress For Success, Put On
the Whole Armor of God

O **The Belt of Truth.** "Stand therefore, having your loins girt about with truth . . ." (Eph. 6:14).

In biblical times the men did not dress for war in pants like we do today. They wore tunics. These were more like dresses. The belt was tied around the waist to lift the hemline up so the soldier would not trip. Not having the belt on might cause you to stumble, and if you stumbled in battle you would be rendered helpless at the hands of your enemy. The Bible says we ought to have on the belt of truth. Have you ever heard someone say, "Why, he tripped over his own lie"? That statement comes from this passage.

Lying is habitual. If you're going to lie you had better have more than one. Mister, if you are going to lie to your wife you had better have more than one lie. Women don't ask questions in packs of one or two. Their questions come in packs of 144 gross. This is not to belittle you ladies. I believe God made you like that to keep us men straight.

Did you know you can lie without lying? Yes. It's called the sin of distortion. You aren't really lying, you're just not telling the truth. For example, my stepfather is a gourmet cook but his mother was not a very good cook at all. So when he eats at someone's home and he doesn't like what they cook he says, "That's just like Momma used to make it." That was a slam and they didn't even know it.

○ **The Breastplate.** ". . . and having on the breastplate of righteousness" (Eph. 6:14).

It would have been near suicidal to go out to battle without your breastplate on. The breastplate covered your heart, your lungs, and other vital organs. The Bible says we ought to put on the breastplate of righteousness. What is righteousness? It is "right living." It's living a life that's in line with God's Word, not the philosophies of this world.

Twenty years ago, if a preacher preached that homosexuality was wrong the congregation would have been in total agreement. There was no debate. And if he preached on abortion, everyone in that congregation would have said, "Amen. Abortion is wrong." Now that same congregation of people hear a message on homosexuality or abortion and many say, "The preacher got off on politics today." But homosexuality is not a political issue. The Word of God condemns it and His word never changes. Neither is abortion a political issue. It's a spiritual issue. Murdering babies is wrong.

The humanist tells us it's all right to abort a baby in cases of rape and incest. They argue, "Why bring a baby into the world if it isn't wanted." Listen, if a baby is in the womb of a woman, it is wanted—maybe not by the woman, but it's wanted by God.

We believe that God is the creator of life and while God hates rape and incest, if conception should occur through these violent acts, He doesn't want that baby aborted. God has a plan for every child's life, regardless of why it was conceived. A perfect illustration is Abraham and Hagar. God had promised Abraham that he and Sarah would have a son. Instead of waiting for the fulfillment of God's promise, Abraham produced a son through Hagar. And even though Ishmael was not God's provision for Abraham, He did not despise the lad but heard the cries of both Hagar and Ishmael when they were facing death in the wilderness.

> . . . for she said, Let me not see the death of the child. And she sat over against him, and lift up her voice, and wept. And God heard the voice of the lad; and the angel of God called to Hagar out of heaven, and said unto her, What aileth thee, Hagar? fear not; for God hath heard the voice of the lad where he is. Arise, lift up the lad, and hold him in thine hand; for I will make him a great nation (Gen. 21:16–18).

Saying that rape and incest are reasons to kill a baby because it isn't wanted, is like saying there is no God! Either life comes from God or it doesn't—that's the real issue. We listen to the humanistic views on abortion until they sound right, but you must understand that humanists do not believe in God as the Creator of life.

○ **The Shoes.** "And your feet shod with the preparation of the gospel of peace" (Eph. 6:15).

The shoes were so important to the children of Israel that God made them last for forty years. Do you know why? Because they had to fight their battles in the hot sand. If you have ever been on a hot sandy beach, you know the importance of wearing shoes.

I've had the privilege through the years of speaking to many professional athletes. I've spoken at chapel services for basketball teams, such as the Boston Celtics, the Atlanta Hawks, the Indianapolis Pacers, and the Philadelphia 76ers. When these seven-foot-tall men come into the chapel service I look at their feet. They do not have average-sized feet. Their feet are huge. Some wear size 18, 20, and even 22. As I looked at their feet I noticed something. They are all wearing basketball shoes. You see, their shoes are designed for playing basketball. They are made for the court.

These gospel shoes are designer shoes, also. They are designed to spread the gospel, and they're not cheap shoes, either. They were purchased with the precious blood of our Lord and Savior Jesus Christ.

○ **The Shield of Faith.** "Above all, taking the shield of faith, wherewith ye shall be able to quench all the fiery darts of the wicked" (Eph. 6:16).

I gather from history that these were not little handheld shields. These were shields the army of Israel would stand behind as the enemy shot their catapults of fire balls. The fire balls would hit the shield instead of the soldiers. The Bible says we ought to have the shield of faith.

Today we are bombarded with the occult. Satan knows exactly what he is doing but we don't have to be fearful and run away. We just need to stand up and fight, and we have the armor to do it, so take the shield of faith. Do you realize that it's impossible to please God outside of faith? It's not just hard, but Hebrews 11:6 tells us it's impossible. This is the reason we cannot give our fear to the Devil. Fear steals our faith.

○ **The Helmet.** "And take the helmet of salvation . . ." (Eph. 6:17).

I believe when a person gets saved he puts on the helmet. Yet most Christians only have on the helmet. I call them "spiritual streakers" because all they have on is a hat and a smile. The Devil is shooting his darts, yet they walk on "naked as a jay bird," as they say where I come from. Yet they are proud of that hat. They can tell you the exact day they got it. If you asked them about the other parts of the armor, they bring you right back to the hat.

Could you imagine someone coming to church with only a hat on? That person would look awfully strange. I wonder how we look when we go out to battle wearing only a hat.

○ **The Sword.** ". . . and the sword of the Spirit, which is the word of God" (Eph. 6:17).

The sword is an offensive weapon. It puts the Devil to flight. He doesn't run from rhetorical preachers. He doesn't flee from philosophical pastors. He is defeated by the Word of God. You cannot beat the Devil with philosophical ideas. He has a masters degree in philosophy. As a matter of fact, he talked one-third of the angels out of Heaven. He is clever. The Word of God is the only level we can use to make sure our homes and lives are straight.

○ **Prayer.** "Praying always with all prayer and supplication . . ." (Eph. 6:18).

The first thing we did in Desert Storm was to send low flying aircraft in to knock out all the enemy's communications. There are two ways the Devil will try to tamper with our communication:

1. **Knock it out.** The first step to backsliding is not lack of Bible reading. The first step to backsliding is not when you miss church. The first step to backsliding is when you stop praying.
2. **Scramble the communications.** If the Devil can't stop you from praying, he will scramble your thoughts as you pray. Have you ever tried to pray for an hour? It's hard. Let me give you a few examples.

   Ladies, have you ever tried to pray for an hour? You start off by saying, "Dear Lord, I thank you because you are the Bread of Life." Then you start thinking, "Bread—I need bread. And don't you know, I'm out of milk, too!"

   And men, you're going to pray for an hour. You say, "Dear Lord, I thank You that You are the Light of the world." Then you think, "Light. You know, the light in the garage has been burned out for two weeks, and I haven't seen my tools for a month. Lord, prepare a place for my son because when I'm finished praying I'm going to send my son to meet you!"

Do you see how Satan scrambles our communication? Today, as never before, we need to put on the whole armor of God, not only for our own protection, but for our homes, as well. May the Lord bless you as you prepare for war.

Thou therefore, my son, be strong in the grace that is in Christ Jesus. And the things that thou hast heard of me among many witnesses, the same commit thou to faithful men, who shall be able to teach others also. Thou therefore endure hardness, as a good soldier of Jesus Christ. No man that warreth entangleth himself with the affairs of this life; that he may please him who hath chosen him to be a soldier (2 Tim. 2:1–4).

MAN'S FIVE
MOST IMPORTANT QUESTIONS

○ **I'm not so bad, am I?**

For all have sinned, and come short of the glory of God (Rom. 3:23).

○ **What is the penalty for sin?**

For the wages of sin is death; but the gift of God is eternal life through Jesus Christ our Lord (Rom. 6:23).

○ **Do I have to clean up my act before God will forgive me?**

But God commendeth his love toward us, in that, while we were yet sinners, Christ died for us (Rom. 5:8).

○ **What must I do to be saved?**

That if thou shalt confess with thy mouth the Lord Jesus, and shalt believe in thine heart that God hath raised him from the dead, thou shalt be saved. For with the heart man believeth unto righteousness; and with the mouth confession is made unto salvation (Rom. 10:9–10).

○ **Could you lead me in a prayer to receive Jesus as Savior?** Yes! Pray this prayer with me now:

Dear Lord Jesus, I know that I am a sinner and I believe that You died on the cross for my sin, that You were buried, and that You rose again. The best I know how, I want to ask You to forgive me of my sin and fill me with Your Holy Spirit that I may serve you the rest of my life, Amen.

Recommended Reading from the Book Shelf

The Family Under Siege, George Grant
Streetwise Parents, Foolproof Kids, Dan Korem
Your Child and the New Age, Berit Kjos
Kids Don't Want To Use Drugs, Dr. Joel C. Robertson
Right From Wrong, Josh McDowell and Bob Hostetler
The New Dare To Discipline, Dr. James Dobson
Like Lambs To the Slaughter, Johanna Michaelsen
Deceived By the New Age, Will Baron

NOTE*J*

Introduction—Missing the Obvious Looking For the Subtle

Chapter 1—Who Prepared the "Chicken Soup"?
1. Tal Brooke, *When the World Will Be As One* (Harvest House Publishing, Eugene, Ore., 1989), 111.
2. Jack Canfield, Paul Klimik, "Education In the New Age," *New Age Journal*, February 1987, 28.
3. Jack Canfield, *New Age Journal*, February 1978, 36.
4. Ibid., 39.
5. Bob Larson, *Straight Answers On the New Age* (Thomas Nelson Publishers, Nashville, Tenn., 1989), 180.

Chapter 2—The Lion Who Would Be King

Chapter 3—Are The Power Rangers Morphing Your Children?
1. Richard Cavendish, *Man, Myth, and Magic* (Marshall Cavendish Co., Long Island, NY, 1983), 1774.

Chapter 4—Power Rangers: The Beasts From Within
1. Bob Larson, *Straight Answers On the New Age* (Thomas Nelson Publishers, Nashville, Tenn., 1989), 67.
2. Richard Cavendish, *Man, Myth, and Magic* (Marshall Cavendish Co., Long Island, NY, 1983), 208.
3. Ibid., 209.
4. Ibid.
5. Ibid., 2819.
6. Ibid., 470.

7. Ibid.
8. Ibid.
9. Ibid., 731.

Chapter 5—Power Rangers: Coloring Their World

1. Samuel Silverstein, *Child Spirit* (Bear and Co., Santa Fe, NM, 1991).
2. Richard Cavendish, *Man, Myth, and Magic* (Marshall Cavendish Co., Long Island, NY, 1983), 430.
3. Texe Marrs, *New Age Cults and Religions* (Living Truth Publishers, Austin, Tex., 1990), 177.
4. Ibid.
5. Richard Cavendish, *Man, Myth, and Magic,* 431.
6. Ibid.
7. Ibid.
8. Ibid., 432.

Chapter 6—Casper, the Unholy Ghost

1. David Benoit, *14 Things Witches Hope Parents Never Find Out* (Hearthstone Publishing, Ltd., Oklahoma City, Okla., 1994).

Chapter 7—Turmoil In the Teepee . . .

1. Willy Peterson, *A New Age Primer* (Unpublished at time of release).
2. *USA Today,* October 9, 1995.

Chapter 8—Indians Coming Out Of the Closet!

Chapter 9—TV Stands For "Transforming Values"

1. Colonel V. Doner, *The Responsible Parent's Guide To TV* (Huntington House, Inc., Lafayette, La., 1988), 16.
2. Linda and Robert Lichter, Stanley Rothman, *The Lichter/Rothman Study,* 17–18.
3. Deborah Sharp, *USA Today,* August 29, 1995.
4. Ibid.
5. Ibid.

Chapter 10—Children Living In a Hostile World

1. Dusty Sklar, *Gods and Beasts, the Nazis and the Occult* (Thomas Crowell Co., 1977), 109.
2. Winkie Pratney, *Devil Take the Youngest,* 133.
3. Ibid., 137.
4. William J. Bennett, *The De-Valuing of America* (Focus On the Fam-

ily, Colorado Springs, Colo., 1994), 111.

5. *The Chicago Tribune,* 1984.

6. Beverly LaHaye, *Who Will Save Our Children?* (Walgemuth & Hyatt Publishers, Brentwood, Tenn., 1990), 193.

Chapter 11—Fleecing the Lambs

1. Josh McDowell, *Right From Wrong* (Word Publishing, 1994), 8–9.

2. Ibid., 9.

3. Dusty Sklar, *Gods and Beasts, the Nazis and the Occult,* 111.

Chapter 12—Who Benefits From Illiteracy?

1. *Forbes,* "The National Extortion Association," June 7, 1993.

2. *Education Week,* June 13, 1985.

3. "Project Literacy U.S. (PLUS)."

4. "Report Card On American Education," 1992.

5. *Blumenfeld Education Letter,* 1991.

6. *Washington Times,* September 10, 1991.

7. David Barton, *America To Pray or Not To Pray,* 1993.

8. Edwin West, *American Education,* January/February 1984.

9. Quote from Al Shanker, president of the American Federation of Teachers.

10. *Blumenfeld Education Letter,* 1991.

11. *Phyllis Schlafly Report,* May 1993.

12. *The Chehalis Chronicle,* November 28, 1992.

13. *The Greenville News,* September 17, 1993.

14. Issue brief from Congressman Dick Armey's office, October 5, 1993.

15. *Phyllis Schlafly Report,* September 1995.

Chapter 13—Origin Distortion, In Search Of the Missing Link

1. Caryl Matrisciana, *The Evolution Conspiracy* (Harvest House Publishers, Eugene, Ore., 1991), 15.

2. Ibid., 17–18.

3. Marlin Maddoux, *America Betrayed* (Huntington House, Inc., 1984), 56.

4. John Dunphy, *Humanist Magazine,* January/February 1983.

Chapter 14—Reasons Why Young People Find Themselves In an "Identity Crisis"

Chapter 15—Suicide: Children Facing the Grim Reaper

1. Jeff Godwin, *The Devil's Disciples* (Chick Publications, Chino, Cal.,

1985), 8.
2. Winkie Pratney, *Devil Take the Youngest* (Huntington House, Inc., Lafayette, La., 1987), 235.
3. Ibid.
4. David Benoit, Harold L. Wilmington, *Battleplan For the Battlefield* (Glory Ministries, Charlotte, NC, 1990), 87–90.

Chapter 16—Suicide, Not a New Problem

Chapter 17—Identifying the Casualties Of This Sexual Revolution

1. George Grant, *The Family Under Seige* (Bethany House Publishers, Minneapolis, Minn., 1994), 24–25.
2. Winkie Pratney, *Devil Take the Youngest* (Huntington House, Inc., Lafayette, La., 1987), 140.
3. Dan Korem, *Streetwise Parents, Foolproof Kids* (Navpress, Colorado Springs, Colo.,1992), 166.
4. Gene Antonio, *The AIDS Cover-Up?* (Ignatius Press, San Francisco, Cal., 1986, 1987), IX.

Chapter 18—The Cross-Dressing Of God

1. Naomi Goldenberg, *Changing of the Gods* (Beacon Press, Boston, Mass., 1979), 82.

Chapter 19—Days Of Our Past Lives: Is Reincarnation Biblically Sound?

Chapter 20—New Age Terms

1. David Benoit, *Fourteen Things Witches Hope Parents Never Find Out* (Hearthstone Publishing, Ltd., Oklahoma City, Okla., 1994), 107–14.

Chapter 21—New Age Symbols

1. Phil Phillips, *Halloween and Satanism* (Starburst Publishers, Lancaster, Pa., 1987), 63–64.

Chapter 22—New Age vs. Christianity

1. Texe Marrs, *New Age Cults and Religions* (Living Truth Publishers, Austin, Tex., 1990), 46–48.

Chapter 23—Dungeons & Dragons: Are Role Playing Games Positive?

Chapter 24—A Parent's Guide To Selecting Children's Programs
1. David Benoit, *Fourteen Things Witches Hope Parents Never Find Out* (Hearthstone Publishing, Ltd., Oklahoma City, Okla., 1994), 107–14.

Chapter 25—Who Will Fill the Gap?

Chapter 26—Overcoming Fear With Faith

Chapter 27—Preparing the Home for Spiritual Warfare

Chapter 28—Man's Five Most Important Questions

Fourteen Things Witches Hope Parents Never Find Out

by David Benoit

For years, witchcraft has been seasonal. It seems every September and October, witches are on bulletin boards, front porches, and windows, as decorations for the upcoming Halloween seasons.

But witchcraft is not just for Halloween any more. Our children are prime targets of these beliefs. Each day children are being preyed upon by witchcraft through the promotion of cartoons, toys, and games.

It has been said, "Those who control the youth, control the future." Could there be a plan in witchcraft to control the future of your child?

ISBN 1-879366-75-4 ● 170 pages